POWERED BY FAITH

POWERED BY FAITH

Pentecostal Businesswomen in Harare

Edited by
TAPIWA PRAISE MAPURANGA

RESOURCE *Publications* • Eugene, Oregon

POWERED BY FAITH
Pentecostal Businesswomen in Harare

Copyright © 2018 Wipf and Stock Publishers. All rights reserved. Except for brief quotations in critical publications or reviews, no part of this book may be reproduced in any manner without prior written permission from the publisher. Write: Permissions, Wipf and Stock Publishers, 199 W. 8th Ave., Suite 3, Eugene, OR 97401.

Resource Publications
An Imprint of Wipf and Stock Publishers
199 W. 8th Ave., Suite 3
Eugene, OR 97401

www.wipfandstock.com

PAPERBACK ISBN: 978-1-5326-6239-3
HARDCOVER ISBN: 978-1-5326-6240-9
EBOOK ISBN: 978-1-5326-6241-6

Manufactured in the U.S.A.   11/26/18

Contents

Acknowledgements | vii

Chapter 1
Introduction | 1
Ezra Chitando

Chapter 2
Background and History of Pentecostalism in Zimbabwe | 8
Fortune Sibanda

Chapter 3
Zimbabwean Women in Business | 29
Nancy Mazuru

Chapter 4
**Postcolonial Zimbabwean Economy:
A Theological Hindsight** | 50
Richard S. Maposa

Chapter 5
**UFIC's 'Victorious Ladies': Using the 'Anointing' to Re-claim
Christian Women's Economic Space in Zimbabwe** | 64
Molly Manyonganise

Chapter 6
**Faith-Driven Business Ladies: Christ Embassy Women
Entrepreneurs in Harare** | 79
Fungai Chirongoma

Chapter 7
Mbiri Kuna Jesu: Pentecostal Women's Economic Participation in Harare: The Case Of Prophetic, Healing And Deliverance Ministries | 96
Tabona Shoko

Chapter 8
Pentecostalism with Profits: An Exploration of Women-in-Entrepreneurship in ZAOGA (FIF) in Zimbabwe | 112
Richard S. Maposa and Tapiwa P. Mapuranga

Chapter 9
Conclusion: Patterns in Pentecostal Women in Business: A Theoretical Exploration of Pentecostalism and Economic Culture in Zimbabwe | 126
Tapiwa Praise Mapuranga

Bibliography | 143

Acknowledgements

FIRST AND FOREMOST, I would like to express my appreciation to CODESRIA for selecting our National Working Group for 2015. Without their financial support, I doubt that this project would really have been carried out in the manner that all group members did. May you continue to support many other such research projects from Zimbabwe and beyond.

As the coordinator, I would also like to express my gratitude to all group members who took their time to go out to the field, and collect crucial information on Women, Pentecostalism and the economic culture in Zimbabwe. This project would not have been there was it not for your commitment and sacrifice. It was definitely not an easy task, but you would agree with me that, "Happiness does not come from doing easy work, but from the afterglow of satisfaction that comes after the achievement of a difficult task that demanded our best"-Theodore Isaac Rubin. Particularly, I would like to mention Fortune Sibanda, Nancy Ziki, Richard Maposa, Molly Manyonganise, Tabona Shoko, Ezra Chitando, Fungai Chirongoma and Chiedza Nyanguru for a job well done. Your contributions will definitely influence policy makers and thus become relevant to contemporary society.

Last but not least, much appreciation also goes to our interviewees who managed to spare some moments to give an ear to our researchers and provide the much needed information for this project. Special mention goes to members of the following ministries: United Family International Church (UFIC), Christ Embassy Church, Zimbabwe Assemblies of God Church (Forward in Faith) (ZAOGA FIF) and the Prophetic Healing and Deliverance Ministries (PHD). I am confident that the information that you gave us was true and unbiased, and is thus quite useful to any researchers on Pentecostalism in Zimbabwe.

CHAPTER 1

Introduction

EZRA CHITANDO

Introduction

ONE KEY DEVELOPMENT ON Zimbabwe's complex religious scene has gone relatively unnoticed: the number of women in business coming from a Pentecostal background. Although scholars have sought to keep up to date with developments in religion in Zimbabwe, Pentecostal women's participation in business has tended to elude their attention. Chapters in this volume seek to address this gap in the available scholarly literature by highlighting the extent to which the Pentecostal gospel of prosperity has inspired, energised and granted legitimacy to women's participation in economic activities in Harare. However, as shall be outlined below, the chapters draw attention to some significant challenges that Pentecostal women in business in Harare face.

This volume represents a very significant development in the study of religion, gender and economics in Zimbabwe. The authors engaged in fieldwork and provide valuable insights into how the Pentecostal movement has enabled many women in Harare to negotiate their entry into spaces that were formerly framed in exclusive masculine terms. Whereas patriarchal ideologies from indigenous cultures and Christianity have been appealed to in order to justify male dominance, the message from the emerging Pentecostal movement has empowered many women to participate in business. Below I highlight some of the key themes that have emerged from the study on Pentecostalism and women in business in Harare.

The Prosperity Gospel as an Enabling Ideology

Studies on African Pentecostalism have identified the prosperity gospel as one major characteristic feature. Scholars have debated the origins of this theology or ideology, with Paul Gifford (1990) initially suggesting that this was a "foreign element." However, David Maxwell (2000) maintained that the creativity of African Pentecostals had to be recognised. On his part, Lovemore Togarasei (2011) has argued that the prosperity gospel in Pentecostalism had positive dimensions, such as motivating individuals to pursue business and investment opportunities. The chapters in this volume highlight this trait, drawing attention to how the different Pentecostal preachers such as Ezekiel Guti of the Zimbabwe Assemblies of God Africa (ZAOGA), Emmanuel Makandiwa of the United Family International Church (UFIC), Walter Magaya of the Prophetic Healing and Deliverance (PHD) Ministry and others have sought to mobilise Zimbabweans to have a positive approach towards wealth.

Chapters that focus on specific Pentecostal churches illustrate the extent to which the prosperity gospel has provided the ideological framework for women to engage in business activities in Harare. Whereas missionary theology and the subsequent mainline church approach has been to emphasise the afterlife, the prosperity gospel concentrates on the "here and now." Believers must not wait to walk regally on the streets of heaven that are paved with gold: they must get their gold now! Different authors have shown how the message of prosperity energises young women, formerly excluded from participating in the mainstream economy, to have the courage to venture into business.

The History of Black Women's Marginalisation in Mainstream Economic Activities

Whilst the prosperity gospel has empowered women to engage in business in contemporary Harare, history shows that black women were largely prevented from participating in the mainstream economy. To say this is not to suggest that black women have been idle, but to draw attention to the effect of colonialism and missionary ideologies of domesticity. When indigenous patriarchal approaches are added to the mix, the net effect is to stifle women's creativity. The portrayal of women as homemakers had the negative effect of limiting their direct participation in business.

Pentecostalism has sought to give impetus to black women's participation in business by maintaining that it is God's will for every believer to prosper. All the negative forces, including ancestral curses, the machination of witches and the scheming of enemies, have no chance against the grace of God poured out to every believer and concretised in material success. Women have latched on to this ideology and have sought to bring themselves from the periphery to the centre. Although they have not yet managed to occupy the most strategic industries (they are mainly concentrated in the informal sector), they have managed to participate in business in Harare (and other centres).

Some chapters in this volume have drawn attention to the extent to which black women have sought to defy the odds by challenging patriarchal domination and engaging in business and investment. Authors have shown how various factors combined to keep women out of participating in business. They have highlighted the struggles that women continue to face as they seek to rewrite history and take their place in the postcolonial economy. As noted above, the Pentecostal gospel of prosperity has contributed towards this shift.

Ambivalence in Pentecostalism's Approach to Gender and Women's Economic Participation

One of the most intriguing dimensions of contemporary studies on Pentecostalism is the ambivalence of the Pentecostal approach to gender. While Pentecostalism seeks to grant space to women, it also limits the scope of women's participation through the notion of male headship. Van Klinken (2013) and Gabaitse (2015) have shown how Pentecostalism enables women to participate actively in various activities. However, they also recognise that there is an underlying assumption that there is a given divine gender order that should not be tampered with. This theology has tended to limit women's full participation in different areas of life.

The chapters in this volume struggle with the ambivalence of the Pentecostal approach to gender in relation to women's economic participation in Harare. Although they acknowledge the positive role played by Pentecostalism in allowing women to take part in business, they also draw attention to how ideas relating to women's supposed subordinate and supporting position have held back many women. They highlight how contentious interpretations of the Bible sometimes result in women being forced to defer to men. In addition, Pentecostal emphasis on the man as the breadwinner and the woman as a "helper/supporter" promotes male dominance in business.

Ongoing Struggle for Women's Economic Empowerment

Alongside the challenges posed by Pentecostal ideologies, some chapters in this volume draw attention to the struggle for the full participation of women in business. These include the need for women to access loans, oppressive cultural ideologies and the absence of an enabling environment. The authors demonstrate that women continue to face challenges in their quest to become more fully engaged in business in Harare. Some authors proceed to provide suggestions as to how to promote the greater involvement of women in business.

While the postcolonial State has sought to improve the status of women through legislation and setting up supportive institutions, women do not yet enjoy equality with their male counterparts. Chapters in this volume have shown how cultural and religious ideologies and oppressive economic policies have combined to force women to remain on the margins. Although the Pentecostal gospel of prosperity has equipped some young women in Harare to engage in successful businesses, many women remain outside, looking in. More work needs to be done by various stakeholders to ensure that women in Zimbabwe become fully involved in social and economic transformation.

Methodology used in this study

The study employs multiple approaches. First and foremost, records of Pentecostal women's participation from specific Pentecostal women's organisations and denominations such as Zimbabwe Assemblies of God Forward in Faith (ZAOGA FIF), Prophetic Healing and Deliverance Ministries (PHD) Christ Embassy Church, United Family International Church (UFIC), amongst others.

Library research is also a major part of data collection. This includes examining published and unpublished documents on women's economic participation in Zimbabwe, as well as the calls for Pentecostal women's participation in business by religious leaders.

Furthermore, Pentecostal and interdenominational conventions where women were encouraged to participate in economic activities were attended (such events are always under way in Harare). Patterns and frequencies were established in selected suburbs and denominations. Crucial respondents included Pentecostal women in business, Pentecostal leaders, economic planners and NGO workers in the field of development work.

Critically, this research involved fieldwork. For five months, the researchers attended Pentecostal women's conventions and interviewed research participants. The research site, Harare, was selected and isolated carefully. Harare constitutes the hub of Pentecostalism in Zimbabwe, with its cosmopolitan outlook and hosting the Head Offices of numerous Pentecostal ministries that are encouraging women's economic participation. Interviews were also held with various categories of research participants who include scholars of religion, media practitioners, politicians and political scientists, civic society and peace activists, religious leaders and members of the public.

In the light of the large numbers involved, Random Stratified Sampling was employed. Respondents were disaggregated to account for race, ethnicity, gender, age, political and religious affiliation, rural/urban residents, as well as socio-economic variables.

Processing and analysis of data included translating some material from Shona and Ndebele and synthesizing data according to themes. Simple statistics, description, comparison, contrast and interpretation were used in the process of interpreting the data.Focus group discussions and in-depth interviews availed qualitative data that helped to clarify the phenomenon under investigation.

There was a direct correspondence between the research objectives and the methodology envisaged. In order to establish Pentecostal women's economic participation in Harare, there was need to enter into the field and gather data on the factors that influence the phenomenon.

Interpretive Framework and Significance

The study is located within the religion and gender paradigm. In particular, it sought to establish whether and how the ideology of Pentecostalism either propels or frustrates women's economic participation. The study avails relevant and critical information relating to the impact of gender ideologies on Pentecostal women's economic participation in Harare. The study has practical significance and its findings have policy implications.

Chapters in this Volume

Seeking to understand the participation of Pentecostal women in business in Harare, the chapters in this volume highlight the underlying role of religious ideologies in engaging in business. However, since religion does not occur in a social vacuum, some of the chapters provide an overview of the historical, political and economic contexts that have given rise to women's participation in business in Harare. In Chapter Two, Fortune Sibanda undertakes a historical overview of African and Zimbabwean Pentecostalism. This enables the reader to appreciate that the current wave of women in Pentecostalism must be placed within the larger narrative of waves of Pentecostalism taking over most spiritual markets. In Chapter Three, Nancy Mazuru provides a detailed analysis of the participation of women in business in Zimbabwe. She describes the empowerment drive championed by the government and highlights the attendant challenges. Richard S. Maposa in Chpater 4 analyses the postcolonial economic history of Zimbabwe. He identifies three distinct phases and illustrates how the economic fortunes have marked each one of these phases. His chapter is strategic in that it enables one to understand how the country's economic history provides the context within which the drama of Pentecostal women in business is played out.

 Having culled the historical context, the chapters that follow proceed to describe the activities of women in specific Pentecostal churches in Harare. In Chapter Five Molly Manyonganise focuses on how the UFIC has energised women to engage in business. She examines the different sources of empowerment that have enabled women to dream big and initiate business activities. However, she also draws attention to some limitations within the movement. Fungai Chirongoma shifts attention to women entrepreneurs in Christ Embassy Church in Harare in Chapter Six. She shows how the publications of the founder, biblical texts and testimonies serve to energise women to participate in business. Tabona Shoko in Chapter Seven focuses on women and economic participation in PHD Ministries. He describes the emergence of the movement and highlights the various economic activities that women in the church undertake. In Chapter Eight, Maposa and Tapiwa P. Mapuranga focus on how ZAOGA mobilises women to participate in business. They outline ZAOGA's guiding theology and how this has assisted many women in Harare to engage in viable economic activities.

As a concluding chapter, Mapuranga identifies patterns in Pentecostal women's participation in business in Harare. Building on the sociological model of the Protestant ethic and capitalism, but applying it to the contemporary situation in Harare, she highlights the trends and patterns in Pentecostal women's involvement in business. Her consistent argument is that the women's faith is critical to their participation in business in Harare.

Conclusion

Although Zimbabwe's economy has been characterised by severe challenges, the resilience of the country's citizens is noteworthy. In particular, the innovation and drive demonstrated by women is salutary. This volume focuses on Pentecostal women's participation in business in Harare. Chapters in this volume explicate the historical context that informs the struggles that women have waged and continue to wage in the quest for space at the economic table. They also provide detailed descriptions of how women in the different Pentecostal denominations in Harare have engaged in business. Further, they critique the limitations of the Pentecostal ideologies and make recommendations regarding additional steps to enhance the full involvement of women in the economy. Overall, the study confirms that women "powered by faith" have sought to shake off the lethargy and engage in business in Harare.

References

Gabaitse, Rosinah M. 2015. "Pentecostal Hermeneutics and Marginalisation of Women," *Scriptura* 114(1), 1–12.
Gifford, Paul. 1990. "African Christianity: A New and Foreign Element in African Christianity," *Religion* 20, 273–288.
Maxwell, David. 2000. "Review Article: In Defence of African Creativity," *Journal of Religion in Africa* 30(4), 468–481.
Togarasei, Lovemore. 2011. "The Pentecostal Gospel of Prosperity in African Contexts of Poverty: An Appraisal,"*Exchange* 40(4), 336–350.
Van Klinken, Adriaan. 2013. "God's World is not an Animal Farm – Or is it? A Catachrestic Translation of Gender Equality in African Pentecostalism," *Religionand Gender* 3(2), 240–258.

CHAPTER 2

Background and History of Pentecostalism in Zimbabwe
FORTUNE SIBANDA

Introduction

THIS CHAPTER PROVIDES AN exploration of the background and history of Pentecostalism in Zimbabwe. This is doubtless, a daunting task because of the intricate religious landscape obtaining on the African continent. Apparently, when John S. Mbiti, the Kenyan-born and pioneering African theologian, remarked in one of his seminal publications that "Africans are notoriously religious" (Mbiti 1969:2), this was purely in defence of African people's religious and philosophical heritage espoused through African Traditional Religions (ATRs), which had been misrepresented, misinterpreted, misunderstood, and displaced by people of other faiths (Mndende cited in Sibanda 2011:13). Nevertheless, today, African religiosity is a world-wide phenomenon both on the African continent and in the Diaspora. Over the years, Mbiti's remark has been confirmed in new guises. On the one hand, there has been a shift in the substantive nature of the African religiosity as the increasing membership of Christians replaced the dominant position of ATRs in the original religious matrix. On the other hand, the relocation of the centre of gravity in Christian circles from the Northern to the Southern Hemisphere (Kalu 2003:215; Sibanda, Marevesa and Muzambi 2013:248) has seen the shift in the numerical strength and spiritual hub of Christianity from the West to Africa, partly due to the rise and development of African Pentecostalism. As Harvey

Cox (1996) asseverates, Pentecostal Christianity is reshaping the 21st century religious landscape.

African Christianity has experienced a phenomenal growth in size and influence noted through the mushrooming of new churches some of which are difficult to describe and categorize in contemporary African society (Gifford 1994:515). On this basis, given that Christianity is not a homogeneous tradition, four broad strands can be identified, namely, Catholicism, Protestantism, African Initiated Churches and Pentecostalism. Pentecostal Christianity currently forms the largest renewal and revival movement within the mainstream Christian faith, which partly explains why it is necessary to interrogate it on a grand scale in the Zimbabwean context. This chapter is largely (but not exclusively) informed by the history of religions approach in order to establish the origins, historical development and impact of Pentecostal churches in Zimbabwe. In addition, the socio-historical, economic and political milieu in which Pentecostalism developed and thrived will be considered in order to situate how the Pentecostal theology, also known as the 'faith gospel', 'gospel of prosperity' or the 'health and wealth gospel' (Togarasei 2011:339), evolved in historical perspective. The chapter also found the gender dimension critical in evaluating Pentecostal women in business so that their voices are heard in movements under male leadership. As part of the background of Pentecostalism, the chapter begins with the definitional challenge of Pentecostalism.

Pentecostalism: The Definitional Challenge

The complex nature of Pentecostalismrequires an exploration into the definitional challenge of what it is. Like most terms in the study of religion, 'Pentecostalism' is elusive to a specific definition. For some scholars, Pentecostalism is defined through some of its elements such as emotionalism, fanaticism, religious mania and the manifestation of the Holy Spirit (Majawa 2007:442). Apart from this, J. Kwabena Asamoah-Gyadu (2005:389) provides a useful definition of Pentecostalism, which can be adopted in this chapter when he writes, thus:

> Pentecostalism may be understood as that stream of Christianity that emphasizes personal salvation in Christ as a transformative experience wrought by the Holy Spirit; and in which such pneumatic phenomena as 'speaking in tongues', prophecies, visions, healing, miracles, and signs and wonders in general, are sought,

> accepted, valued, and consciously encouraged among members as evidence of the active presence of God's spirit.

The view expressed above shows the centrality of the Holy Spirit among the believers who expect incorporation into Christ after being born again through water and spirit baptism. The importance of the spirit baptism to ensure that one is 'spirit-filled' cannot be underrated in Pentecostal churches as it mirrors Jesus' advice to Nicodimus when he said that "no one can see the kingdom of God unless he is born of water and spirit" (John 3:5). On this basis, Pentecostal churches and denominations claim their mandate from the biblical Pentecostal experience recorded in the book of Acts. However, this chapter takes cognizance of the fact that not all Pentecostal churches stress the manifestation of the gifts of the spirit such as *glossolalia*, notwithstanding that Pentecostalism is sometimes referred to as "the born-again movement" (Maxwell 1998:350). Closely related to the concept of Pentecostalism is the term 'charismatic', derived from the Greek word *charis* or *chairen*, which in English is 'charisma' and refers to "God's gift granted to an individual" (Majawa 2007:155). On this basis 'charismatic' can be defined as the low-key Pentecostal renewal movements that operate in the mainline Protestant denominations or even the Roman Catholic Church (Gifford 1988:4; Majawa 2007:20). Stating the type of distinction and relationship between these two terms is vital in showing the influence of Pentecostalism on the religious plane in Zimbabwe. Furthermore, Togarasei (2011) says that Pentecostal churches are also called modern Pentecostals or the charismatic Pentecostals to distinguish them from classical or missionary Pentecostalism that sprouted from the Azusa street experiences. This helps to shed light on the typologies of Pentecostalism, which forms the focus of discussion in the next section.

Understanding the Typology of Pentecostalism

In the long and complex history of the Pentecostal phenomenon, one can identify the diverse terrains and typology of Pentecostalism. Broadly speaking there is 'classical Pentecostalism' which tends to be a western phenomenon and 'African Pentecostalism', which is the African expression of a global Pentecostal movement. However, Kalu (2003:222) identifies the emphases which form ten types of Pentecostal movements as follows: "inter-denominational fellowships, evangelistic ministries, deliverance, prosperity gospellers, Bible distribution, Children ministries, rural evangelism, intercessors for Africa, classical Pentecostal missions from Europe and charismatic movements in various mission churches." It is not surprising that the focus of these different movements have some overlaps as well as some distinctive elements on the basis of theology and practices. In this chapter some of the types of Pentecostalism highlighted above will be covered in more detail because of their relevance to the study. The inter-denominational aspect is relevant when discussing the Evangelical Fellowship of Zimbabwe (EFZ) women's gatherings during the 'decade of crisis', where women were challenged to pull down ethnic walls, initiate change through hard work and entrepreneurship in face of socio-economic challenges in Zimbabwe (Biri and Togarasei 2013:85). In addition, prosperity gospellers are also a critical shade of Pentecostal movement that also overlaps with classical Pentecostalism and African Pentecostalism. We now turn to the latter two streams of Pentecostalism.

Classical Pentecostalism in Historical Perspective

Classical Pentecostalism is the type of Pentecostal movement that manifested through missions in Europe and the United States of America (USA). For Richard Nenge, Molly Manyonganise, Onias Dehwa, Richard Maposa, and Alben Muchererwa (2013:113), the word 'Pentecostal' in the western context was used in reference to the older 'classical' Pentecostals who emerged as a result of the Azusa street revival in Los Angeles, USA, between 1906 and 1908. Pentecostalism in the USA is said to have emerged in the early 1900s. According to Nontando M. Hadebe (2013:115), the history of the Pentecostal church began with Charles Parham (1873–1929) when he baptized Agnes N. Ozman with the Holy Spirit. This particular baptism resulted in making Ozman to speak in tongues. Speaking in tongues was significant because, first, it proved that baptism of the Holy Spirit was a separate experience after conversion. Second, it revealed that speaking in tongues was evidence of the baptism in the Holy Spirit. Third, it proved that gifts of the spirit, signs, wonders and healing were endemic to the church and did not end with the Early Church, Jesus or the apostles. The second figure credited for influencing the emergence of Pentecostalism was William Seymour (1870–1922). Seymour was an Afro-American preacher and former student of Charles Parham (Hadebe 2013). According to Cecil M. Robeck cited in Nontando Hadebe (2013:115), through the 'Azusa Street Mission' (1906–1908), people "spoke in tongues, prophesied, preached divine healing, went into trances, saw visions, and engaged in other phenomena such as jumping, rolling, laughing, shouting, barking, and falling under the power of the Holy Spirit." These developments are essential in understanding the nucleus of Pentecostal beliefs and practices.

The early group of Pentecostals was made up of people from diverse racial, cultural, class, age and gender divides. In terms of class, the early Pentecostals consisted of the "socially marginalized, politically voiceless, economically deprived and ecclesiastically slighted group" (Hadebe 2013:115). Pentecostals believe that these early members were powered by faith, given voice and status by the Holy Spirit. Because of the Azusa Street mission, evangelists and missionaries were sent out all over the USA and throughout the world beginning from 1907. Nontando Hadebe (2013:116) noted that these Pentecostal missions emphasised "restorationalism, revivalism, divine healing, sanctified holy living or a 'higher life' and millenarianism." The growth of Pentecostalism in the USA was a world record as it started as a prayer group of fifteen people to become an international ministry in space of three months. There are over 500 million Pentecostal adherents the world over and the majority of them are found in Latin America, Asia and Africa (Hadebe 2013). With Africa claiming the second largest share of Pentecostals, we now turn to a historical overview of African Pentecostalism.

A Historical Overview of African Pentecostalism

The African continent is also a theatre with diverse experiences of the Pentecost. African Pentecostalism refers to the Pentecostal churches that are identified as an African expression of the global Pentecostal movement, which constitute a growing form and new factor in Africa Christianity. In terms of its origins, Ogbu Kalu posits that "Pentecostalism in Africa has indigenous roots while it has benefited from external interventions and spiritual flows" Kalu 2003:220). This shows that African Pentecostalism was a local initiative. Beginning in the second half of the 20th century, African Pentecostalism has experienced a phenomenal growth to become one of the most significant expressions of African Christianity (Nenge et. al. 2013:113). Along the same lines, Ogbu Kalu (2003:220) and Lovemore Togarasei (2011:338) aver that the African Pentecostals are a new wave of churches that emerged in the 1970s, building up on the pre-1970 spiritual flares, some of which influenced this spiritual revival.

According to Ogbu Kalu (2003:221, 222), African Pentecostalism had different periods with related spiritual dynamics, which are explored in further detail here. First, in the pre-1970s, the indigenous prophets responded to colonial Christianity through charismatic movements; Second, the 1970s saw a spiritual revival particularly among the youth in secondary schools and tertiary institutions showing charismatic gifts in different countries including Zimbabwe; Third, in the 1980s, Pentecostalism experienced further growth through the efforts of the Faith Movement and Faith Gospellers at a time when some African economies collapsed and human rights abuses were rife, thereby making Pentecostalism more attractive as a religion of the oppressed. Fourth, in the 1990s, prosperity gospel was under public attack, as the born-again were called to resort to the 'holiness emphasis of old'. Fifth, in addition to Kalu's historical account of African Pentecostalism, there is the contemporary period stretching from 2000. In Zimbabwe, this period coincided with the Zimbabwe crisis and witnessed the emergence of new churches such as United Family International Church (UFIC) and the Pentecostal Deliverance and Healing (PHD) Ministries that appealed to the poor and the rich, young and the old due to miracles of different types. The chapter returns to this element later under the section on Pentecostalism in Zimbabwe. The major principles of Pentecostalism are discussed in the next section.

Cardinal Elements of Pentecostal Thought and Practice

Pentecostal thought and practice is heterogeneous. Different churches tend to stress different elements, but there is a common ground that forms the nucleus. According to Togarasei (2011:338), Pentecostal churches are "characterized by transnationalism and internationalism, association with urban areas, preaching of gospel of prosperity, spiritism and association with modernity." In this section, focus zeroes down on two of these characteristics, which shed more light on the contribution of women in business powered by faith. The first element is that of spiritism. Pentecostalism places special emphasis on the direct personal relationship with God through the baptism of the he Holy Spirit. As such, the Day of Pentecost (Acts 2:1–4) where the Holy Spirit was experienced by the disciples of Jesus is regarded as the watershed of Pentecostalism and a cardinal element for all believers. On this basis, humanity is divided into the redeemed ('the born-agains') and unredeemed, the former constituting the spirit-filled people manifesting spiritual gifts such as *glossolalia* (speaking in tongues), prophecy, healing, exorcism and deliverance, among others. The Pentecostal church model regards the encounter with the power of God in Jesus as very critical and such an experience is expected to produce objective results as evidence of renewal, healing and spiritual transformation. Spiritism can be a basis of Pentecostal women to initiate change, nation-building and sustainable development.

The second element is that of the gospel of prosperity. A theology anchored on the 'faith gospel' of health and wealthis central in Pentecostal churches and very critical in evaluating the role of Pentecostal women in business at the centre of this study. Historically, the faith gospel is regarded as an American doctrine designed by media evangelists in the 1950s and 1960s (Gifford 1994:516). Similarly, David Maxwell (1998:350) and Lovemore Togarasei (2011:339) observe that the 'gospel of prosperity' was the brainchild of American preachers such as E.W. Kenyon, Oral Roberts, Kenneth Hagin as well as Kenneth and Gloria Copeland. It developed in the USA as an apology for the wealth which was acquired and fed into the capitalist economy (Mapuranga, Chitando and Gunda 2013:302). However, this is not a universally acclaimed position that scholars such as David Maxwell (1998:351) noted about ZAOGA that prosperity gospel teachings emerged from the Southern African sources and in turn shaped by the Zimbabwean milieu. The main thrust of this gospel is its emphasis on prosperity as a product of faith, but there are different versions to the gospel of prosperity. It is said that poverty is a result of the devil and a disease which one needs to be delivered from. In ZAOGA, for instance, the processes of social and economic transformation are anchored on the doctrine of talents and the Spirit of poverty (Maxwell 1998:355). Through talents believers are encouraged to use their hands to survive and to transform their status from being employed to become employers. Prosperity is also understood on the basis of health. Tabona Shoko (2008) is amongst the scholars who have contributed on the health and wealth gospels by using the case of healing in Hear the Word Ministries in Zimbabwe. On the whole, to get healthy or wealthy, one needs to 'sow seeds' of prosperity by giving to the church in order to be blessed (Togarasei 2011:341). Notably, the widespread nature of poverty in Africa has become a fertile ground for the emergence of Pentecostalism in Zimbabwe.

The Rise and Development of Pentecostalism in Zimbabwe: A Historical Reflection

There are different factors that are credited for the rise and development of Pentecostalism in Zimbabwe. In general, there are both push and pull factors to the development of Pentecostalism, but these are not exclusive to each other. On the whole, the Pentecostal churches appealed to many people because it declared a *kerygma* for Africa and Zimbabwe that placed God's ability to resolve people's spiritual, physical and material problems (Nenge et. al. 2013:115). As part of the pull factors, the new Pentecostal churches introduced effective strategies that attracted Christians from historic mainline churches. Pentecostal churches denounced mainline churches for practicing 'dead religion' (Gifford 1994:526), which Asamoah-Gyadu (2005:409) similarly referred to as "staid, silent and cerebral Christianity of the mission churches." Therefore, the Pentecostal explosion of the 1980s happened at the expense of the mainline churches, which were regarded as spiritually weak. As such, in this earlier wave, many young people were absorbed by the new Pentecostal churches at an alarming rate.

In line with the above, the Pentecostal churches' performance of divine signs such as Spirit baptism with tongues, the healing of all kinds of illnesses as well as deliverance from all forms of evil forces, whether spiritual or social, attracted many people in Zimbabwe. The Pentecostal churches addressed the spiritual needs of the people through performing healing miracles (Kalu 2003). This greatly appealed to people who were suffering, poor and marginalised in society. As more and more people testified at crusades and other platforms for being healed and delivered from the grip of Satan, poverty, witchcraft, evil spirits and barrenness, this increased the relevance of the 'born-again' movement in the country. The Pentecostal churches have become a pragmatic and powerful 'third force' with spontaneous responses to a ready audience, irrespective of social status, gender, age, race and level of education, as opposed to the 'intellectualized gospel' of western missionaries deemed superficial.

The Pentecostal churches propagated a 'full gospel' through different methods of evangelization to fulfill the Pentecostal mission of converting many souls to Christ in the shortest possible time. The Pentecostal worship sessions and crusades have emotional intensity and aggressive evangelism meant to reach out to the 'lost' in the power of the Holy Spirit (Majawa 2007:437; Nenge, et. al. 2013:113). As Ogbu Kalu (2003) observes, the

Pentecostal model of 'power evangelism' is anchored on the "triple task of re-evangelisation, intensification and reconstruction of Christian experience. The media and modern technology are exploited to convey the new experience and millenarian theme and weave together the rural, urban and global contexts." Indeed, the churches of the Pentecostal fold in Zimbabwe exploited the opportunities granted by the information society and local popular culture to consolidate their goals. The youth are particularly attracted by the use of modern musical instruments such as the guitar, key board and the public address system. This had an impact on people who felt empowered in church circles. Harvey Cox cited in Nenge, et. al. (2013:114) posits that "the great strength of the Pentecostals lay in the ability to combine its aptitude for local languages, the music cultural artifacts and to adjust to the setting in which they found themselves." Thus, they have managed to indigenize and contextualize their approach and message in the Zimbabwean context.

The Pentecostal churches are 'people of the book' on the basis of their significant dependence on the Bible and for utilizing large amounts of printed materials, newsletters, pamphlets and books, audio-visual cassettes , posters and stickers as well as electronic media like television and radio (Kalu 2003:223). In addition, the Pentecostal churches in Zimbabwe make use of social media networks such as Facebook, Twitter and Skype to reach out to their audience. This is why Lovemore Togarasei (2011:338) says that the Pentecostals make good use of the public media to advertise their services and other church activities. The televangelism fever has gripped many Zimbabwean Pentecostal churches some of whom now use satellite television. The Pentecostal churches that broadcast through satellite television in Zimbabwe include, among others, Christ TV of Emmanuel Makandiwa's UFIC, Yaddah TV of Magaya's Prophetic Healing and Deliverance ministries, Miracle TV of Eubert Angel's Spirit Embassy and Ezekiel TV of Ezekiel Guti's ZAOGA FIF (Muranganwa 2014).

The 'Zimbabwe economic crisis' is one of the challenges in Zimbabwe the led to the emergence of Pentecostal churches in the country. The magnitude of the crisis was so great to the extent there was untold suffering in the economic, social and political spheres. In the words of Maxwell Kadenge and George Mavunga (2012:153) the crisis was characterised by, among other things, "steep declines in industry and agricultural productivity; historic levels of hyperinflation; informalization of labour; dollarization of economic transitions; displacements; and critical erosion of livelihoods."

During the first decade the New Millennium research has established that women were among the worst affected by the socio-economic turmoil, but they 'survived the urban jungle' (Mapuranga 2014) powered by faith in order to fend for their families. Arguably, this contributed to the rise of new Pentecostal churches in the country. Therefore Pentecostalism, in general and Pentecostal gospel of prosperity in particular became a coping strategy to survive the socio-economic challenges. This was one of the pull-push factors that saw people turning to Pentecostalism in their numbers. In the words of Lovemore Togarasei (2010:19) the "post-colonial religious, political, economic and social developments have given birth to elitist Pentecostal churches referred to in the vernacular as *chechi dzemucheno* (churches for the smartly dressed) or *chechi dzevapfumi* (churches for the rich)." These churches are the new havens for the marginalised and the emerging black elite class in post-colonial Zimbabwe.

Cartography of Pentecostal Churches in Zimbabwe

There are diverse strands of Pentecostal churches in Zimbabwe, which can be categorized diachronically and synchronically. Therefore, the history of religions approach becomes handy in order to describe the different phases. Most of these churches have become trans-national in nature. Despite this success, one may still ask in wonder: If all these churches are powered by the same faith, why are there a multiplicity of Pentecostal Churches in Zimbabwe? What is the place of women in these churches? In order to map out the main Pentecostal churches in Zimbabwe, they can be grouped into three historical epochs, viz: the pre-colonial phase (pre-1980); the post-colonial phase (1980–2000); the New Millennium phase (since 2000). Brief details are provided for each phase, tabulating the basics such as the founder, contexts and circumstances that saw the rise of these different Pentecostal churches in Zimbabwe.

Phase I: the pre-colonial period up to 1980

In the early phase, the main examples of Pentecostal churches that come to mind are the Apostolic Faith Mission (AFM) and Zimbabwe Assemblies of God, Africa Forward in Faith (ZAOGA FIF). For Lovemore Togarasei (2010:20,21) AFM was founded in Zimbabwe as part of the efforts of people like the evangelist Zacharias Manamela who worked in Matabeleland region around 1915, Enock Gwanzura who was baptized around 1930, and L. Kruger, a white missionary who revived AFM in the 1930s and preached in the reserves around Harare. Another important figure was Rev. Morgan J. Sengwayo. Sengwayo is sometimes regarded as the founder and Overseer of the Apostolic Faith Churches in Central and Southern Africa between 1955 and 1981 (Carver 1987:1). Sengwayo once worked in South Africa before operating in Zimbabwe as a clerk and part-time preacher in Harare before moving to Gweru. In 1954, he turned to full time ministry assisted by his wife in order to preach the word of God in the same way as the apostles of the early church. Through visions he received, Sengwayo said he was commanded not to lean or depend on anyone, black or white (Carver 1987:1). This is the basis of self-reliance and hard work that believers were expected to follow. Some of the operations of AFM have been a cause of struggle that led to expulsions from the church. The current President of AFM in Zimbabwe is Dr A. Madziyire supported by a set of male National Overseers, showing gender imbalances on positions of power in the church.

Nevertheless, in AFM, there is evidence of women empowered by faith. The AFM in Zimbabwe website shows that from the four major conferences held by the church annually, two of them are significant in the context of women empowerment. Under the Ladies Ministry or Ladies Department, there is on the one hand, the Women's Conference that has existed for over 100 years and attended by over 50 000 women across the country. On the other hand, the Widows and Single Mothers (WISMO) conference established in 1997 in Harare by Rev. Murefu and headed by Amai Josphine Madziyire who is wife to the current church President, is attended by over 7000 members of the church. WISMO is important because it encourages "members to be self-sufficient in order to take good care of their families through teachings, prayer and projects" (www.afminzimbabwe.com). In addition, the Ladies Department contributes "financially to the Kingdom of God, through projects which complement the Sisters Union" (www.afminzimbabwe.com). This shows that the women in the church virtuous women (cf. Prov. 31:10–13) powered by faith to support and sustain families and finance various church projects against all odds.

Ezekiel Handinawangu Guti and Eunor Guti are at the helm of the ZAOGA FIF. This is largely an urban movement that originated in Harare (then Salisbury). Gifford (1994:515) says ZAOGA was founded in the 1950s and first experienced a significant growth in the 1970s, during the Second Chimurenga, and further grew in the late 1980s. David Maxwell (1998:351) notes that ZAOGA was found by a group of young entrepreneurs in 1959 including Ezekiel Guti, Abel Sande, George Chikova, Joseph Choto, Raphael Kupara, Kennedy Manjova, Clement Kaseke, Lazarus Mamvura, Aaron Muchengeti, Priscilla Ngoma and Caleb Ngorima after being expelled by AFM missionaries. This group briefly joined the South African Assemblies of God under Nicholas Bhengu from which they were again expelled to then form the Assemblies of God, Africa (AOGA), now ZAOGA (Maxwell 1998). Therefore, the claim that Guti was the sole founder of ZAOGA is nullified. The contribution of Priscilla Ngoma on the doctrine of talents has been the basis of teaching women to 'prosper the church' and themselves by using their hands. Popularly known as *matarenda*, the doctrine of talents is a theology of self-liberation where congregants are encouraged to 'seed' money in order to get blessings. This has seen many ZAOGA women and youth in business such as cross-border trading, selling food stuffs and clothes, among other things. Some other women like Fungisai Zvakavapano-Mashavave ministered through gospel music with messages of resilience powered by faith in times of economic turmoil. Though marginalised, Pentecostal women during the crisis years initiated change through interdenominational forums, which encouraged hard work and entrepreneurship (Biri and Togarasei 2013). This has also been confirmed by the findings of David Maxwell (1998:356) when he writes, "Although men and children also volunteer for talents [,] it is predominantly a female activity." This suggests that women, who form the majority in ZAOGA, are powered by faith and are a force to reckon with in a movement that has become transnational comprising over a million followers in Zimbabwe alone, and many other adherents found in other countries in Africa, Europe and America.

Phase II: the Post-Colonial Period (1980- 2000)

The onset of this period coincided with the political independence of Zimbabwe. The new political dispensation allowed a wider interaction of people across the racial, age, gender and class divide, which was a fertile ground for Pentecostal churches to thrive, particularly with government's open policy on freedom of worship. The Pentecostal churches of this period covered in this section are the Celebration Ministries International (also known as Hear the Word Ministries) and the Family of God (FOG) Church. In the long history of its existence, the founders of Celebration Ministries

Pastor Tom and Bonnie Deuschle are given credit for establishing a church that initially operated as the Rhema Bible Church. Tom Deuschle originally came to Zimbabwe from the USA on 20 February 1979 with a view to preaching the word of God in the country as a sole missionary. After visiting the USA in 1981, Tom met and got married to his wife Bonnie. Upon return to Zimbabwe and after visiting South Africa they began a church in their living room of their house with six people in April 1982 (www.celebrate.org/celebration-churches; Togarasei 2010:23). Today, Celebration Ministries International has its headquarters in the posh suburb of Borrowdale Park and over 85 churches globally in Zimbabwe, UK, USA, South Africa, Kenya and Australia, among others. Their focus on work of the Holy Spirit, gospel of prosperity and faith healing has endeared the church to black and white congregants from the middle class. The church operates through various ministries meant to address the needs of the urban poor (Togarasei 2010). The Tom and Bonnie Deuschle case, like others, shows the active participation of women in the ministry, despite the fact that gender equity remains a forlorn ideal.

Andrew Wutawunashe established his Family of God (FOG) Church together with a group of youth in 1981 in Harare. Initially, the church operated under the tag of the Witness Ministries. FOG was a result of a breakaway from the Reformed Church in Zimbabwe, a mainline church perceived as practicing a spiritually 'dead religion' (Gifford 1994:526). The 'young zealots', as David Maxwell (1998) describes those who rebelled from historic churches, began to stress "the idea of being born-again, speaking in tongues and the performance of miracles" (Togarasei 2010:23). The church soon established branches in other urban centres of Zimbabwe such as Bulawayo, Gweru, Mutare and Masvingo. In the mid-1980s, FOG church became international as branches were opened in central and southern African countries as well as outside Africa including the Ireland, UK and USA (Togarasei 2010:23). Shuvai Wutawunashe, the wife to Andrew Wutawunashe became very popular for ministering through gospel music where she is sometimes regarded as the 'mother' of gospel music in Zimbabwe. As a gospel music artist, Shuvai Wutawunashe mirrors the element of Pentecostal women in business.

Phase III: the New Millennium Period (since 2000)

The beginning of the third phase is marked by the post-colonial economic and political challenges that bedeviled Zimbabwe, but which saw the increased popularity and development of new mega-churches. Indeed, the turn of the new millennium witnessed the birth of new prophetic indigenous churches under leaders who were "young, male and polished" (Chitando, Manyonganise and Mlambo 2013:153). However, some of the healing episodes and the versions of the gospel of prosperity in these new churches made people to wonder whether the so-called prophets were 'men of God' or 'men of Gold' on the basis of what has been termed 'gospreneurship' or 'gospelneurship', a new art of spinning money in the church (Guvamombe 2012). The main churches covered are Mathias and Mildred Ministries, United Family International Church (UFIC) and the Prophetic Healing and Deliverance (PHD) Ministries. Mathias and Mildred Ministries was founded and is run by Mathias and Mildred Madzivanzira. The ministry was very popular between 2005 and 2009 because of their 'miracle healing' claims during the Zimbabwe crisis. They established the Rock Chapel Assembly in Zimre Park near Ruwa. However, their fame plummeted because of satanic allegations that saw the shooting and killing of their worker under mysterious circumstances. It is believed that the worker had seen a snake vomiting money in their house in an act linked to Satanism (The Zimbabwe Situation 2014). The case of Mathias and Mildred Ministries underscores the need for people to 'believe not every spirit, but try the spirits'. The fact that this church was named after the founders, Mathias and Mildred, suggests that there is a semblance of power sharing in the leadership.

The United Family International Church (UFIC) was founded by Emmanuel Makandiwa in August 2008 in Harare as a breakaway group from AFM where he was a pastor prior to launching of this church (Mapuranga, Chitando and Gunda 2013:301). The followers are attracted by the gospel of prosperity that promises believers both health and wealth. Miracles and prophecies were some of the major landmark attractions of UFIC which received intense media coverage in recent years. Some of Makandiwa's miracles attracted a lot of debate, which left people wondering whether these were "miracles or magic" (Sibanda, Marevesa and Muzambi 2013:256). For instance, through the electronic media, there were testimonies to the fact that Makandiwa performed some miracles which resulted in 'miracle money', 'miracle baby', 'miracle weight loss', among others. Emmanuel Makandiwa closely works in his ministry with his wife Ruth Makandiwa, who has invested heavily in charity projects to assist the needy. The prophetess, Ruth Makandiwa leads the UFIC women in business under the 'Victorious Ladies' forum. There is a lot of bureaucracy in UFIC to the extent that people are grouped according to the amounts they give in the church. Those who give less are marginalised whilst those who give more are accorded front seats in services with easy access to the leader and presumably blessings when they are 'showered' by the 'Man of God'. Apparently, the majority of women continue to be strategically marginalised in the church due to poverty that disqualifies them from positions of gender equality. Today, UFIC is found in different cities in Zimbabwe and is one of the most populous international churches with adherents in Africa, Europe and America.

Walter Magaya's Pentecostal Healing and Deliverance (PHD) Ministries is one of the most recent Pentecostal churches in Zimbabwe having been founded in 2012 in Harare. His spiritual father is T.B. Joshua of the Synagogue Church of All Nations. Like Makandiwa's UFIC, Magaya's church is a crowd puller that has attracted people from far and wide. Through the charismatic leadership of Magaya, PHD has become a platform for winning souls and mapping a new avenue of economic emancipation through miracles (The Zimbabwean Situation 2014). However, Magaya is not immune to controversies surrounding his ministry partly because of his 'permissive ethics' in which he has tried to lure converts who are engrossed in weird lives such as prostitutes. Some expressed skepticism on his miracles and the source of his power. Magaya uses 'anointing oil', which he began selling to his congregants in 2014 on the pretext that it would unlock a new lease of life punctuated by health and prosperity. Magaya's wife is referred to as 'Mother' in the church. Today Magaya's church is also an international mega church with members from all over the world. Therefore, the Pentecostal ministries have become popular because they promise material salvation through the gospel of prosperity.

The Role of Pentecostal Women in Business Powered by Faith

This section analyses the participation of Zimbabwean Pentecostal women in business ventures. A gender approach is adopted as a tool of analysis. The motive is to reflect on the socio-economic status of women in historical perspective and their implications for the future of Pentecostal churches in Zimbabwe and beyond. It has to be asked: How far liberative are Pentecostal churches to women in their business ventures? Is the 'gospel of prosperity' really empowering to all women or it is a façade that adequately caters for the aspirations of the prophets' wives and founders of the churches? Is Pentecostalism the opium of the oppressed women? The whole issue is ambivalent. What comes to mind is expressed in two levels.

The first level is the endemic gender disparity that continues to dominate the Zimbabwean credoscape. The Shona adage which says "*Kwadzinorohwa matumbu, ndikwo kwadzinomhanyira*" (literally, where they have their stomachs beaten is where they rush) may be appropriated in Pentecostal church contexts with reference to women in business. Some of the challenges that Pentecostal women encounter include poverty, low social status and lack of formal leadership positions in the church, deprivation and exclusion from public privileged spaces that are gendered in favour of men such that most women are located at the margins. Doreen Massey's (1994:15) explanation of a 'gendered space' is instructive to what obtained to most Pentecostal churches in Zimbabwe. She regarded 'gendered space' as the socially constructed, geographical, and architectural arrangements and space, which regulate and restrict women's access to spaces that are linked to the "production of power and privileges in a given context." In most churches the male gender enjoyed a superior position at the expense of their female counter parts. Therefore, it can be argued that women efforts have been exploited by male leadership to line their pockets. On this basis, the metaphor of a 'carrot and stick' method mirrors the gender relations in these churches.

Despite being the most numerous in church and the most hardworking under the pretext of working talents, instanced by ZAOGA, women have not been accorded a chance to fully enjoy the fruits of their labour of love and faith. This evokes a 'hermeneutics of suspicion' coined by Paul Ricoeur and usefully adopted by feminist theologians to critique gender disparities in society. Indeed, when space is gendered women look for a language that expresses their aspirations and hopes through group identities in economic and spiritual contexts. As Mapuranga (2014:232) rightly notes, the status of women continues to be "a status of struggle, a struggle to survive collectively and individually against the cultural and traditional realities in their society." This is a historical fact that calls for the self-awareness of women to resist all forms of oppression and dehumanization as they remain "perpetual beasts of burden" (Sibanda and Maposa 2013:143) in these churches with 'gendered spaces'. However, there is hope for transformation because Doreen Massey (2005:9) was insightful when she asserts that space "is always in the process of being made. It is never finished; never closed." This can catapult women in business to greater economic heights.

At the second level, in most Pentecostal churches in Zimbabwe, as discussed in other sections of this chapter, women were portrayed as partners and not mere submissive wives in the ministries established by the male founders. This is related to the positive developments in Africa's New Religious Movements as observed by Rosalind Hackett (1995:262) when she writes in this regard:

> Africa's new religious movements provide a rich and varied spectrum of women's agency. Religious symbols and practices shape women's perceptions of themselves, their relations with other, their ability to act, and provide strategies for survival and empower and disempower them within the context of their religious and wider communities.

The above quotation implies that if women believe in themselves, they can realize a full economic and social liberation that is independent of men. For example, in ZAOGA, despite the fact that Eunor Guti is a late comer and not a co-founder of the church, she has been entrusted with authority comparable to that of Ezekiel Guti. She has shown her abilities through healing, preaching and prophesying, and has been accorded titles of honour such as Prophetess and Archbishop, just as her husband. Eunor Guti is a force to reckon with in ZAOGA, spiritually and in circles of economic empowerment.

In addition, in ZAOGA, it can be asserted that the initiation of women in the matrix of evangelism and business by Prophetess Archbishop Eunor Guti shows that she has successfully "bargained with patriarchy" (Mapuranga 2012:74). Women are beginning to come out of the traditional 'cacoons' where they were regarded as "delicate, frail and totally dependent on men" (Moila 2002:16). This was done through reversing traditional methods that presented "men in the pulpit and women in the pew" (Hendriks et. al. cited in Mapuranga, Chitando and Gunda 2013:317). Thus, some women have excelled in other ministries of the church showing their contribution. In addition, Eunor Guti as a prophetess of high acclaim is the brainchild of the famous Women in Business Forum, which is an interdenominational platform where Pentecostal women and those from other churches were exhorted to work hard through engaging in entrepreneurial ventures for social and economic empowerment. This creative effort is being fine-tuned to include all women participants irrespective of race or creed for the sake of atrophying the disempowerment they suffered through oppressive masculinities. The scenario explains why Biri and Togarasei (2013:79) argued that Pentecostal women contributed to the transformation and nation-building in the face of socio-economic challenges in Zimbabwe.

In some Pentecostal churches gospel music is a vocation and strong instrument for evangelism and economic empowerment particularly for women gospel artistes. According to Fred Zindi (2003:6) "Music is the most powerful of all art forms. No other form of expression is as direct as influential. It has the potential of self-expression and reaching others directly. It is the strongest social weapon for fighting any battles." Perhaps, this is the type of mentality that has inspired the women gospel artistes who have gone beyond participating in church choirs to recording and releasing commercial gospel albums, notwithstanding that the music industry was by and large considered as a male domain in Zimbabwe. In fact, contrary to the popular view that the music industry is an occupation for *marombe* (the layabouts) only, a number of Zimbabwean female gospel artistes have taken their music as business. These include, among others, Olivia Charamba of AFM, Ivy Kombo of ZAOGA FIF, Shuvai Wutawunashe of FOG and Fungisai Zvakavapano-Mashavave of ZAOGA FIF. Notably, in 2003, Ivy Kombo received the National Arts Merit Award (NAMA) in the category of Best Selling Gospel Artiste ahead of Prince Mafukidze and Fungisai Zvakavapano-Mashavave (Zindi 2003:132, 133). Therefore, the women musicians were able to praise the Lord and to make money through music. There is no doubt that music ensures that congregants are kept inspired and educated on the word and the need to work hard in order to attain self-empowerment, spiritually and materially through the gospel of prosperity.

Conclusion

The chapter has demonstrated that Pentecostalism is a diverse and complex phenomenon that has attracted huge crowds of people in contemporary Zimbabwe. Its history is long, diverse and tortuous. From the main types of Pentecostalism, it is that African Pentecostal theology that has appealed to the Africans, in general and Zimbabweans in particular because of its meaning and relevance to their existential circumstances of the economic crisis that pauperized, displaced and seriously eroded the livelihoods of many people. Amongst the worst affected were women who turned to religion in their large numbers for solace. This partly explains why Pentecostal churches arose and developed in different historical periods largely as an urban phenomenonin Zimbabwe. Through the gospel of prosperity these churches have touched the nerves of the people's spiritual, economic and physical needs. Powered by faith and "the will to arise" (Oduyoye and Kanyoro 1992), the Pentecostal women, who form the majority of membership in Pentecostal churches, ascended against all odds created by the 'Zimbabwe economic crisis' to initiate change through hard work, hope for blessings and empowerment by the faith gospel. Therefore, it can be concluded that in spite of the Pentecostal patriarchal 'vice-grip', women are fast becoming like the very stones that the builders once rejected in business from time beyond reckoning as their agency make them cornerstones for sustainable development in Zimbabwe.

References

Asamoah-Gyadu, J.K. (2005) "'Born of Water and the Spirit': Pentecostal/Charismatic Christianity in Africa" in: O.U. Kalu (Ed.) African Christianity, pp. 388–409, Available on: http://repository.up.ac.za/bitstream/handle/2263/21579/016_Chapter15_p388-409.pdf?sequence=17, Accessed: 10 March 2015.

Biri, K. and Togarasei, L. "'. . .but the one who prophesies, Builds the Church': Nation Building and Transformation Discourse as True Prophecy: The Case of Zimbabwean Pentecostal Women" in: E. Chitando, M.R. Gunda and J. Kugler (Eds.) *Prophets, Profits and the Bible in Zimbabwe*, Bamberg: UBP, pp. 79–94.

Carver, L.C. (1987) "The Founding of the Apostolic Faith Work in Zimbabwe and its Growth in Southern Africa" Available on: www.hatnews.org, Accessed: 20 April 2015.

Chitando, E., Manyonganise, M., and Mlambo, O. (2013) "Young, Male and Polished: Masculinities, Generational Shifts and Pentecostal Prophets in Zimbabwe" in: E. Chitando, M.R. Gunda and J. Kugler (eds.) *Prophets, Profits and the Bible in Zimbabwe*, Bamberg: UBP, pp. 153–170.

Cox, H.G. (1996) *Fire from Heaven: The Rise of Pentecostal Spirituality and the Reshaping of Religion in the Twenty-First Century*, Reading: Addison-Wesley.

Gifford, P. (1994) "Some Recent Developments in African Christianity," African Affairs, Vol. 93 (373), October, pp. 513–534.

Gifford, P. (1988) *The Religious Right in Southern Africa*, Harare: Baobab Books.

Guvamombe, I. (2012) "Gospreneurship – Are they looking for God or Gold?," *The Herald*, 13 September.

Hackett, R.I.J. (1995) "Women and New Religious Movements in Africa," in U. King (ed.) *Religion and Gender*, Oxford: Blackwell, pp. 257–290.

Hadebe, N.M. (2013) "Healing and HIV in Pentecostal Churches" in: E. Chitando and C. Klagba (Eds.) *In the Name of Jesus!: Healing in the Age of HIV*, Geneva: WCC Publications, pp. 111–129.

Kadenge, M. and Mavunga, G. (2011) "The Zimbabwe Crisis as Captured in Shona Metaphor," *Journal of African Cultural Studies*, Vol. 23(2), Dec., pp. 153-164.

Kalu, O.U. (2003) "'Globecalisation' and Religion: The Pentecostal Model in Contemporary Africa" in: J.L. Cox and G. ter Haar (Eds.) *Uniquely African?: African Christian Identity from Cultural and Historical Perspectives*, Trenton: Africa World Press, Inc., pp. 215-240.

Majawa, C.C.A. (2006) *The Holy Spirit and Charismatic Renewal in Africa and Beyond: Pneumatological Considerations*, Nairobi: Creations Enterprises.

Mapuranga, T.P. (2013) "Bargaining with Patriarchy?: Women Pentecostal Leaders in Zimbabwe,"*Fieldwork in Religion*, Vol. 8(1), pp.74-91.

Mapuranga, P., Chitando, E., and Gunda, M.R. (2013) "Studying the United Family International Church in Zimbabwe: The Case for Applying Multiple Approaches to the Study of Religion and Religious Phenomena," in: E. Chitando, M.R. Gunda and J. Kugler (eds.) *Prophets, Profits and the Bible in Zimbabwe*, Bamberg: UBP, pp. 299-321.

Mapuranga, T.P. (2014) "Surviving the Urban Jungle: AICs and Women's Socio-Economic Coping Strategies in Harare (2000-2010) in: E. Chitando, M.R. Gunda and J. Kugler (Eds.) *Multiplying in the Spirit: African Initiated Churches in Zimbabwe*, Bamberg: UBP, pp. 227-239.

Massey, D. (1994) *Space, Place and Gender*, Cambridge: Polity Press.

Massey, D. (2005) *For Space*, London: Sage.

Maxwell, D. (1998) "'Delivered from the Spirit of Poverty?': Pentecostalism, Prosperity and Modernity in Zimbabwe," *Journal of Religion in Africa*, Vol. 28(3), pp. 350-373.

Moila, P.M. (2002) *Challenging Issues in Christianity*, Pretoria: Unisa Press.

Muranganwa, T. (2014) "Free-to-Air Decoders: Televangelists Worst Affected," *News Day*, 22 July.

Nenge, R., Manyonganise, M., Dehwa, O., Maposa, R. and Muchererwa, A. (2013) *History of Christianity in Africa*, Harare: ZOU.

Oduyoye, M.A. and Kanyoro, M.R.A. (1992) *The Will to Arise: Women, Tradition and the Church in Africa*, New York: Maryknoll.

Sibanda, F. (2011) *African Blitzkrieg in Zimbabwe: Phenomenological Reflections on Shona Beliefs on Lightning*, Saarbrucken: Lambert Academic Publishers.

Sibanda, F., Marevesa, T. and Muzambi, P. (2013) "Miracles or Magic?: Theological Reflections on the Healing Ministry in Pentecostal Churches in Zimbabwe" *JIARM*, Vol. 1 (8) September , pp. 248-261.

Sibanda, F., and Maposa, R.S. (2013) "Beasts of Burden?: Women in HIV & AIDS Contexts in the United Church of Christ in Zimbabwe," in: E. Chitando and S. Chirongoma (Eds.) *Justice not Silence: Churches Facing Sexual and Gender-based Violence*, Stellenbosch: AFSA, pp.133-144.

The Zimbabwe Situation, (2014) "Disgraced Pastors Back on the Prowl," 23 July.

Togarasei, L. (2010) "Churches for the Rich? Pentecostalism and Elitism" in: L. Togarasei and E. Chitando (eds.) *Faith in the City: The Role and Place of Religion in Harare*, Uppsala: Swedish Science Press, pp. 19-39.

Togarasei, L. (2011) "The Pentecostal Gospel of Prosperity in African Contexts of Poverty: An Appraisal," *Exchange*, Vol. 40, pp. 336-350.

Togarasei, L. (2011) "The Pentecostal Gospel of Prosperity in African Contexts of Poverty: An Appraisal," *Exchange*, Vol. 40, pp. 336-350.

www.afminzimbabwe.com/AFM_conferences.html, Accessed: 23 May 2015.

www.afminzimbabwe.com/ladies.html, Accessed: 23 May 2015.
Zindi, F. (2003) *The Pop-Music Work Book: Zimbabwe Versus the World*, Harare: Zindisc Publications.

CHAPTER 3

Zimbabwean Women in Business
NANCY MAZURU

Introduction

IN ORDER TO PUT Pentecostal women's participation in business in Harare, it is important to have an appreciation of women's role in business. This chapter sets out to outline the history of Zimbabwean women in business. The number of women embarking into business is increasing globally, both in developed and developing countries. It is generally agreed among many scholars that women entrepreneurship is making a significant improvement on women's lives and is contributing to economic growth in many countries across the globe. Women entrepreneurship is becoming more important, especially in developing countries, as it contributes to employment creation, as well as increasing household incomes especially in times of economic stagnation. In developing countries, forty to fifty percent of enterprises are owned and run by women (Mboko and Smith-Hunter 2009). The same authors further argue that in Zimbabwe, there is high participation of women in business, especially at micro-level though others are formalising and growing their business beyond survival level. Pentecostal women are among women entrepreneurs in Zimbabwe who are making significant strides towards their economic empowerment. Most of these women have a strong belief of being powered by faith in their business endeavour. Women entrepreneurs in Zimbabwe are found both in rural and urban areas. In urban areas, women engage in business activities such as street vending, while others run grocery shops, flea markets boutiques and restaurants. Others, though very few, have more formalised companies which provide goods and services. In rural areas, women also perform business activities such as gardening, poultry and piggery cooperatives and others run grocery shops. However, a significant number of women entrepreneurs in Zimbabwe are found in urban areas, as compared to rural areas.

Background of women in businesses in Zimbabwe

In the developing countries, particularly those in Africa women have faced many years of discrimination economically, socially and politically. As noted by Chapamba (2010:64), women are victims of systematic prejudice, including discriminatory laws, policies, financial constraints and years of neglect socio-culturally, educationally and legislatively regarding business. The discrimination against women in Zimbabwe, together with gender inequalities, can be traced back to the pre-colonial and colonial eras and this was largely due to patriarchal structures of many African societies which are deeply embedded in their culture. Historically, women were regarded as child bearers and carers and their place, as noted by Kanyenze (2011: 211) was in the kitchen, while men were regarded as bread winners. Kanyenze further avers that colonialism strengthened patriarchy as it required men to work in the newly created mines, farms and emerging towns, while women remained in the poor rural areas, and this, in a way, motivated them to join the liberation struggle.

Due to several types of discrimination faced by Zimbabwean women, they were economically sidelined for many years. It was difficult for them to get formal employment and entrepreneurial opportunities. The world of business has been predominantly a masculine domain in many countries (Luppinacci 1998:4). Zimbabwe is not excluded from these countries. However, it is important to note that in independent Zimbabwe, various organisations and associations which aimed at improving the socio-economic status of women were formed and women themselves were the main advocates. These include, the Indigenous Business Women's Organisation, Women in Business and Skills Development in Zimbabwe and the Zimbabwe Women's Resource Centre and Network (ZWRCN) (Kanyenze 2011:210). All these aimed at involving and increasing women's participation in the economic sphere.

Because of these organisations and other related associations, women have expanded their entrepreneurial base in Zimbabwe. The government of Zimbabwe demonstrated its commitment to the advancement of women by signing a number of regional and international conventions, treaties and protocols, including the convention on Economic, Social and Cultural rights, the Convention on the Elimination of all forms of discrimination against Women (CEDAW), the Beijing Declaration and Platform for Action and the 1997 SADC Declaration on Gender and Development among others (Statement by H.E Chitsaka Chipaziwa, Ambassador and Permanent Representative of the Republic of Zimbabwe to the United Nations on Agenda 28: Advancement of Women). These protocols and treaties had direct and indirect impacts on improving women's participation in business as they all help to reduce and eventually eliminate the various forms of discrimination faced by women, which sometimes affect their involvement as well as their active participation in entrepreneurship.

The government of Zimbabwe also created ministries which have roles to play in increasing and improving women owned businesses, though sometimes indirectly. The Ministry of Women's Affairs, Gender and Community Development is one of these ministries and it aims at empowering women through policies, strategies and programmes that promote their participation in national development. Related to the above is the Ministry of Small to Medium Enterprises and Cooperative Development which aims at providing skills and management training that support entrepreneurship and small business growth. This ministry also aims at poverty alleviation, employment creation in rural areas and empowerment of the previously disadvantaged (Msipah et al 2013:83). Thus, the two ministries have a role to play on women's entrepreneurship advancement in that through the former ministry, women's empowerment through policies, strategies and programmes provides them with a platform to start their own business and helps those already in business to expand their activities, thereby increasing women's participation in national development. The later ministry, through its aim of supporting small to medium enterprises, as well as empowering the previously disadvantaged groups, helps in paving the way for the emergence and growth of women-owned businesses, considering the fact that women were also among the groups that were previously disadvantaged in business and employment. According to Chopamba (2010:64) the general outcry by most African women when it comes to their socio-economic marginalisation has prompted Zimbabwean women to do something practical about rectifying the situation and the solution is entrepreneurship, which has long been recognised as a key factor in the economic empowerment of women. It is also against this backdrop that the number of Pentecostal women in business increased as they believed that through being powered by faith, their businesses would prosper, thereby helping them to come out of poverty.

Women business activities in Zimbabwe

Women in Zimbabwe are engaged in several types of businesses both in the formal and informal sectors. However, it should be noted that the majority is in the informal sector doing small businesses. The informal sector is more expansive in Zimbabwe these days because of the economic meltdown being experienced in the country. The economic recession of Zimbabwe started in the 1980s and stretched into the early 1990s following the adoption of the Economic Structural Adjustment Programme (ESAP) by the government of Zimbabwe (Ncube 2000:161). Zimbabwe's ESAP resulted in increasing unemployment, characterised by decrease in real wages (Munyikwa 2009:63) These crises accelerated at the turn of the new millennium, leading to the closure of many companies (Chiweza 2010:14). More than 400 companies had closed during 2000 (Europa publications: 1236). The number further increased as the economic depression worsened, notably between 2007 and 2008. Even at the time of the study and writing (2015), companies were still closing down, thereby further increasing the unemployment rate. Retrenchments, as noted by Chiweza (2013:14) were the order of the day in the country, with up to 80 per cent unemployment. Because of this, the number of women business activities, especially those in the informal sector, increased. Some of the business activities performed by Zimbabwean women are as follows:

Cross-border trading

Chitando (2004:24) notes that when the economic situation in Zimbabwe deteriorated in the 1990s, there was a marked increase in the volume of cross border trading. Quite a significant number of women in Zimbabwe are cross border traders and they go to places such as South Africa, Botswana, Zambia, Malawi, Tanzania and Dubai where they import several types of goods such as clothes, blankets, kitchen ware, curtains, and groceries. Some were going to Mozambique where they imported bales of second hand products, especially clothes. Sibanda and Maposa (2014:220) assert that cross border traders in Zimbabwe exported goods which had high demand in countries such South Africa and Botswana that include mats, tie and die cloths and agricultural products such as legumes that include *nyimo* (roundnuts), *nzungu* (groundnuts) and *mufushwa* (dried vegetables). The same authors also argue that on the other hand there are also some import goods which included household items such as fridges, stoves and television sets radios, clothes, blankets and groceries which are far much cheaper in these neighbouring countries as compared to the same goods manufactured locally.

It is important to note that among these cross border traders were women in Pentecostal and African Independent Churches. Chitando (2009:31) states that enterprising women who were active in the informal sector visited prophets in the hope of boosting their sales and that other women received holy water which they sprinkled on their goods for the cross border trade. Chitando further argues that some women could have their passports sanctified by prophets so that they would not be deported. These women had faith and hope that prophetic power could help them make substantial progress in their businesses. Thus, their businesses were based on faith. The imported goods were sold in flea markets, in streets or in boutiques. Many cities in Zimbabwe such as Harare, Masvingo, Bulawayo, and Mutare among others have boutiques which are owned by women. It should be noted that in most cases, boutiques can eventually expand and become formalized.

Salons

Hairdressing is improving the living standards of many women in Zimbabwe. Although this service can be offered at residential areas, a significant number of women are opening up hairdressing shops (salons). Most of the salons in Zimbabwe are run and owned by women. Some owners of these salons have employees, while others work for themselves, depending on the size of the salon and the clientele base. In these salons, women can also sell hair accessories such as weave and braids and cosmetics such as lipstick, cutex, artificial nails and other small items such as handbags. Data from interviews carried out in Masvingo and Harare reveal that most hair salons charge a minimum payment of US $10 and a maximum of US $30 per hair do. Quite a significant number of salon owners and their employees indicated that they belong to Pentecostal group of churches such as Zimbabwe

Assemblies of God Africa (ZAOGA), the Apostolic Faith Mission (AFM) and Christ Embassy among others. Pentecostal churches encourage their members to be always presentable, hence most women and girls value fashionable clothes, flashy hair styles and showy make up. Probably, they borrow this concept from biblical sources which say "cleanliness is close to godliness"(Leviticus 15, Matthew 23:26). This has caused many Pentecostal women to embark on the business of hairdressing because they have a strong base of clients from their church mates. This is different from other groups of churches such as African Independent Churches like the *Johane Masowe* and the African Apostolic Churches of Paul Mwazha and Johane Marange which encourage women to always cover their heads and avoid make-ups. Perhaps these churches have also borrowed this concept from (1 Corinthians 11:6) which says:

> "If a woman does not cover her head, she should have her hair cut off, and if it is a disgrace for a woman to have her hair cut or shaved off, she should cover her head."

Hence the teaching on looking smart and presentable has opened business avenues for Pentecostal women in Zimbabwe.

Restaurants

The selling of fast foods has been increasing in many urban areas of Zimbabwe. Women were opening up restaurants where they sold cooked food such as sadza, rice, fresh chips, burgers and pies. A lot of people who work in towns buy their lunch from restaurants and most of them prefer sadza. This is largely because sadza is the staple food in Zimbabwe and is cheaper as compared to other types of foods such as fresh chips and burgers. A survey carried out on many restaurants in Harare reveals that the price for a plate of sadza ranges from a minimum of US $1 to a maximum US$3 depending on the location of the restaurant. Restaurants which are located downtown are cheaper as compared to those located in the CBD. Most of the restaurants located downtown get their clients from vendors, commuter omnibus crew (drivers, conductors and rank marshals), those who sale at flea markets and many people who are employed in low paying jobs.

Grocery Shops

Historically the running of grocery shops was a male domain. However, women nowadays are also participating in this business. The groceries which are sold are either manufactured locally or internationally. Women can import groceries such as cooking oil, soap, flour and other items such as pampers. In most cases, these grocery shops are operated in town centres and residential areas. It is important to note that some women are running these grocery shops as joint ventures with men. For example Food World Supermarket started as a tuck-shop jointly owned by Innocent Chisvo, his brother and his wife Joyce in 1985 in Chitungwiza, Harare (entrepreneurshipafrica 5 December 2011). However, some women in rural areas are also running their own grocery shops.

Gospel Music Business

Some Zimbabwean women have embarked on the business of gospel music. Gospel music, as noted by King (2012: 8), has become a multi-million dollar industry and as a result, many people have constructed their businesses around this particular ministry. Prominent women gospel musicians in Zimbabwe include Olivia Charamba, Fungisai Zvakavapano-Mashavave, Mercy Mutsvene, Shingisai Suluma and Joice Simeti among others. Most of the women in the business of gospel music are members of the Pentecostal churches. Unlike other types of music or businesses, gospel music is not associated with unethical activities or conduct, hence most parents and husbands allow their daughters and wives respectively to partake in this business. Besides that, these gospel musicians tend to have fans from their fellow church mates, members of other Pentecostal churches and the general public. Chitando (2002: 65) asserts that a number of music tracks in Zimbabwe maintain that the lives of converts to Christianity are characterised by prosperity. This theme is dominantly coming from evangelical/Pentecostal churches, although it occurs in the compositions from mainline and African independent artists (Chitando 2002: 65). Chitando further states that there is an observable link between the gospel of prosperity found in Zimbabwean gospel music and the theme of providing ethical guidelines. Most of gospel singers, as noted by Michael (2005), are blatantly in the business for money.

Clothing manufacturing

Clothing manufacturing is also another business activity dominated by women in Zimbabwe. If properly managed, this business has the potential to grow, despite the fact that it usually starts as a small business. Women involved in this business engage in sewing several types of garments, including casual clothes, school uniforms, sofa covers, curtains and bedroom ware. In some cases, manufacturers of these clothes open up clothing shops or sell their products to retailers and wholesalers in bulk. Marvellous Designs, located at corner Albion and Mbuya Nehanda St in Harare, is an example of a clothing manufacturing shop owned by a woman. This enterprise is owned by Marvellous Bakesa and it specialises on sewing garments, particularly African attire (Interview with Marvellous Bakesa, 20 March 2015, Harare). Some women in Harare are doing this type of business at their homes. Bemac Fashions in Greendale, Masasa is a very good example. This business which specialise in sewing women clothes including sofa covers and African attire is owned by a woman called Blessing Machingauta (Interview with Blessing Machingauta, 19 March 2015).

Foreign Currency exchange

Foreign currency exchange has become a vibrant economic activity in Zimbabwe. Although men are also participating in this business, the number of women seems to overweigh that of men and they are earning a living, as well as empowering themselves through money changing. The most common currencies which they normally deal with are the South African Rand and the United States Dollar and in other cases the Botswana Pula. Although this business is regarded as illegal in Zimbabwe, many people still engage in this type of business. In Bulawayo women of the Apostolic church who usually dress in white clothing have been in this type of business for decades. Foreign currency exchange has improved the lives of these women, together with other women from all over Zimbabwe who are in the same type of business. During the period between year 2000 and 2008, when Zimbabwe experienced a serious economic crisis, many people who were in the business of foreign currency exchange were making gainful profits since the Zimbabwean dollar was losing its value almost every day. Demand for foreign currency was very high because many people avoided keeping their money in local currency because of the hyperinflation. On the other hand, the number of people who were engaged in cross-border trading increased as this was the most common alternative of earning a living. Others were crossing borders to buy groceries for their families. Because of this, the demand for foreign currency increased in Zimbabwe and those who were in this business benefited a lot. They made huge profits, especially during public holidays such as Christmas and Easter when many people in the diaspora came home. Some even bought big assets such as houses and cars while others made investments and opened up other new businesses. Foreign currency exchange was deeply rooted in *chikorokoza*, a Shona name referring to illegal business practices. Even in the years after 2008, women are still doing this type of business, though it is no longer viable as it used to be. This is largely because of the dollarization of the economy which was introduced by the government in 2009, which saw Zimbabwe using multi currencies, notably the South African Rand and US dollar. These currencies are stable and it is therefore difficult for people in this business to make high profit these days.

Cooperatives

Co-operatives are common in Zimbabwe. Women are joining co-operatives where they make joint ventures in business, especially in income generating projects such as poultry and gardening. Co-operatives are usually common in rural areas but are also increasing in urban areas. Non-Governmental Organisations (NGOs) and governments usually support the emergence and growth of women cooperatives. Even in towns, NGOs such as Action Contre La Faim are drilling boreholes and facilitating gardening co-operatives. This enables women in these co-operatives to sell their vegetables and other products in order for them to earn a living.

It is important to note that most of these business activities are classified under the category of small enterprises. Although there are wide variations on the criteria used to categorise small, medium or large enterprise, there seem to be a general consensus among many scholars that a small enterprise employs less than 50 workers, medium sized enterprises employ between 50 and 199 and large enterprises employ 200 and more (Abdullah and Bakar 200:185). Basing on the above criterion, it is clear that although women's businesses are growing in Zimbabwe, most of them are still small enterprises as they do not employ many workers. A survey carried out on several businesses in Zimbabwe shows that business activities such as salons have number of employees ranging from 1 to 8, while most restaurants have a minimum of 2 and a maximum of 6.

However, there are other groups of women, though very few, who are expanding their business from small enterprises to medium enterprise, up to large enterprise. Bauer (2013) avers that there is a small but emerging group of business women who are becoming industrialists, for example by running their own gold mines, but little is known about the range and limits of their economic activities. Although most of Zimbabwean women businesses are largely found in the informal sectors and small enterprises, what is interesting to note is that many Zimbabwean women are entrepreneurs.

Disparities among Zimbabwean Women in Business

An important point to note when discussing women entrepreneurship is that they are not a homogenous group (Mboko and Smith-Hunter 2009). In Zimbabwe women entrepreneurs have different backgrounds and they are influenced by different factors to start their own businesses. They also have different aspirations when doing their businesses. Firstly, their levels of education differ. Some women in business have high levels of education to the extent that some have tertiary qualifications. Others have low levels of education to the effect that some of them do not have secondary education. Most of the women with low levels of education are more into vending activities. However, with the increasing shrinking of the Zimbabwean economy, even women with high levels of education are also becoming vendors. Moreover, due to different levels of education, some of the women in business are formally employed and they take entrepreneurship as an extra-income generating activity, while others are not employed and they only rely on their businesses for survival. Female teachers, nurses and other civil servants are examples of formally employed women entrepreneurs. They sometimes engage in cross border trading where they import goods for sale, either at their workplaces or employ some people who sell these products at flea markets or in boutiques. Education increases the chances of getting employment. In this regard, most women with low levels of education rely on their business activities as the main source of income because their chances of getting formal employment are limited.

Religious denominations also differentiate Zimbabwean women in business. It is important to note that most women in business belong to different churches even though they can be put in similar brackets such as Pentecostal churches or African Independent churches or mainline churches. More so, not all women in business are Christians, some belong to the religion of Islam and they normally run boutiques and sometimes formalised clothing shops. Thus in this regard, Pentecostal women who are the focus of this book belong to different churches such as ZAOGA, UFI ministries, AFM, Christ Embassy among others, hence, they are not homogeneous to some extent.

Marital status is another important factor which distinguishes Zimbabwean women entrepreneurs. Historically, businesses, such as cross border trading were dominated by single mothers who were usually household heads. Married women were forbidden or discouraged by their husbands to do this type of business as it was usually associated with prostitution. Muzvidziwa (1998: 30) alluded to the point that there was a negative portrayal of female cross-border traders, especially by the media. Women cross-borders were portrayed as having prostituted themselves with haulage truck drivers and also blamed for spending long periods in South Africa selling nothing but their bodies. Muzvidziwa further argues that, this explains why some widows were not allowed to get passports by their late husbands, who believed that cross-border trading was not fit for married women. However, as the economy of Zimbabwe continued to shrink down, the negative portrayal of female cross-border traders as prostitutes gradually changed and many husbands are now allowing their wives to partake in this business. Just like women in cross-border trading, women who worked in hairdressing shops were also negatively portrayed as prostitutes but these perceptions have changed as many married women are also working in salons or run their own salons. There is a growing realisation among Zimbabwean men that married women can make significant improvements in household income through their small businesses. Because of this, a notable number of men in Zimbabwe are now allowing their wives to participate in small businesses and some even give financial support to their wives so that they can start their own businesses. Married women in Zimbabwe are supplementing their husbands' incomes through their own businesses while some single mothers are also earning a living from their businesses.

Area of residence is also another factor which shows that female entrepreneurs are heterogeneous in Zimbabwe. As has already been discussed, some female entrepreneurs reside in rural areas, while others reside in urban areas. In this regard they encounter different opportunities and different constraints. Usually, women businesses in rural areas are affected by the remoteness of the area, for example some rural areas are far away from towns and cities. They often suffer from poor infrastructural development, which in turn affects their businesses, especially in cases where there are transport problems due to poor roads, women in business face challenges of transporting their products to market places. In addition, women entrepreneurs in rural areas suffer more from financial constraints and they have limited chances of expanding their businesses as compared to those in urban areas.

Factors influencing the growth of female entrepreneurship in Zimbabwe

Globalisation has a role to play in as far as the growth of women owned businesses is concerned in many parts of the world including Zimbabwe. Schech and Haggies (2000:58) cited by Porter *et al* (2008:128) define globalisation as the intensification of global interconnectedness, a process which they see as associated with the spread of capitalism as a production and market system. As argued by Zeidan and Bahrami (2011: 100), women entrepreneurship started to gain momentum first in the countries where women were gaining access to professional opportunities and equal rights with men during the second half of the 20th century. However, as the world started to move towards an information age with internet, cell phones and satellite TV in the centre of people's life, even in far corners of the planet and as the pace of globalisation increased, women in developing countries joined the race to start their own businesses, even in some traditional societies. Some Pentecostal women indicated that they were inspired by the entrepreneurial progress made by other Pentecostal women in other countries through watching television. Thus, globalisation enables women everywhere especially in developing countries to be motivated by women's business activities in other countries especially through televisions, thereby inspiring them.

As already been discussed, the government of Zimbabwe enacted several pieces of domestic legislation designed to promote gender equality and the empowerment of women since independence including the Legal Age Majority Act of 1982, Labour Relations Act of 1985, the Matrimonial Causes Act of 1985, the Sexual Discrimination Removal Act, the Sexual Offences Act of 2001, the Domestic Violence Act of 2007 and the National Gender Policy of 2004 (statement by H.E Chitsaka Chipaziwa,

Ambassador and Permanent Representative of the Republic of Zimbabwe to the United Nations on Agenda 28: Advancement of Women). The same report further states that the government enacted a National Gender Policy Implementation Strategy and Work Plan for 2008-2012 which provides guidelines and the institutional framework to engender all policies, programmes and projects and activities at all levels of the society and economy. All these acts passed by the Zimbabwean government removed barriers that were limiting women's employment and empowerment opportunities, thereby opening up avenues for Zimbabwean women to enter the world of entrepreneurship.

Moreover, the United Nations Millennium Development Goals have also influenced the growth of women owned businesses in Zimbabwe. Zimbabwe was among the 189 Heads of State and Governments, which agreed to the Millennium Declaration at the Millennium Summit of September 2000. (Zimbabwe Millennium Development Goals, 2004 progress report). The Millennium Development Goals (MDGs) have a role to play in as far as the advancement of women entrepreneurship is concerned in Zimbabwe, especially MDG3 which aims at promoting gender equality and empowering women. The target of this goal is to eliminate gender disparity in primary and secondary education, preferably by 2005 and at all levels by 2015 (Todaro and Smith 2011: 24). Zimbabwe has made significant progress in narrowing gender disparities in both primary and secondary education (Zimbabwe Millennium Development Goals, 2004 progress report). It is important to note that addressing gender disparities in the education sector offers women the opportunity to empower themselves and increase their entrepreneurship skills. Education is, therefore, an important ingredient of entrepreneurship and entrepreneurship itself is also an important ingredient of women empowerment which in turn leads to development.

Although women entrepreneurship in Zimbabwe can be traced several years back, it should be noted that the number of women owned businesses increased since the beginning of the second millennium up to the present day, mostly because of the economic constraints. Zimbabwe faced serious economic challenges since the turn of the second millennium. As indicated earlier in this chapter, the cirises which had started during the 1980s increased during the 1990s due to the failure of the ESAP which was adopted by the government of Zimbabwe in 1990 (Ncube 2000: 161, Munyikwa 2000: 63). The crises were further worsened by the government's handing out of huge unbudgeted Z$ 50 000 individual pay offs to the liberation war veterans which came to an estimated total of Z$4 billion and Zimbabwe's involvement in the Democratic Republic of Congo's civil war in September 1997 (Sachikonye 2002:15, Doxtader and Villa-Vicencio 2003:192–194). The 2000 land reform programme that transferred farms from the from minority white commercial farmers to majority landless blacks exacerbated the economic down turn (Sachikonye 2002:15, Brown 2008: 269) As a result of the deepening economic crises, the manufacturing sector was tremendously affected, leading to the closure of many companies and the subsequent high rates of unemployment. This was further worsened by a decrease in real wages (Munyikwa 2000:63). By the summer of 2007, Zimbabwe's inflation rate was the highest in the world, reaching 3,000 percent annually (Brown 2008: 269). The cost of a household monthly basket rose from Z$686, 116 in February to Z$1, 483, 324 in March 2007 (Brown 2008:271).

Due to the slowing down of the economy, coupled with increasing unemployment, women business activities in Zimbabwe also increased in order to cope with the situation. Women's business activities are important because they improve household earnings. The World Intellectual Property Organisation (WIPO) cited by Hussan and Mugambi (2013:47) states that during the years of economic crisis and recession, one robust sector that provides economic growth, increases productivity and employment is that of small and micro enterprises. More than 50 percent of Zimbabwean women entrepreneurs who were interviewed indicated that they were forced by harsh economic conditions to start their own businesses. Women-owned businesses are playing a more active role in society and the economy, representing about 25.8–28% of entrepreneurs in the world (Markovic 2007).

Although results from several interviews carried out among women business owners revealed that their prime aim was to get income for earning a living and improve their economic empowerment, some married women indicated that they wanted to liberate themselves from depending on their husbands' income. Besides its income generating role, business ownership contributes to a person's equilibrium and sense of fulfilment (Coughlin and Thomas 2002:4). Self-esteem, according to Todaro and Smith (2011:21) is a second universal component of good life and it is a sense of worth and self-respect, of not being used as a tool by others for their own ends. In this regard, some women engage in entrepreneurship in order to gain economic freedom. Coughlin and Thomas (2002: 13) also argue that almost universally women who are into business want to gain more independence and achieve recognition. Most of the single mothers interviewed indicated that they have been denied the opportunity to be self-reliant by their late or divorced husbands, hence participation in business enables them to be economically independent.

The importance of supporting women owned businesses in Zimbabwe

Women constitute a greater percentage of the total population of Zimbabwe. In 2012, the total population of the country was 12 973 808, with 6 738 877 women and 6 234 931 males (Zimbabwe National Statistics Agency (ZIMSTAT), 2012 Report: 1). The proportion of male and female population was 48% and 52% respectively (Zimbabwe Statistics Agency, 2012 Report: 1). Women constitute a greater percentage of the people in poverty, not only in Zimbabwe, but globally. It is estimated that women constitute 70% of the poor people in the world (Report by the Organisation for Economic Cooperation and Development (OECD) to the United Nations Commission on Sustainable Development). In Zimbabwe, women's poverty is exacerbated by the fact that women constitute a greater percentage of the unemployed population. A survey carried out by ZIMSTAT in 2011 revealed that although women's share in the labour force has increased over the years, the gap between the percentage of women in paid employment and that of men remains wide. The same survey showed that 31 percent of the economically active men were in paid employment compared to 14 percent females. In this regard, women owned businesses serve as an alternative to employment creation among women. Women entrepreneurship is increasingly being recognised the world over. Developing and supporting women owned enterprises enables women to meet their current needs, augment their earnings and acquire resources for future investments (Chao 1999:29). Women owned businesses helps women to improve their living conditions, as well as boosting the economy. (Vossenberg 2013:1) notes that women entrepreneurs have been designated as new engines for growth and the rising stars of the economies in developing countries to bring prosperity and welfare. In Zimbabwe, women businesses are important because of the following reasons:

Firstly, women are primary care givers in Zimbabwe, just like in many developing countries. Although several steps have been undertaken to promote gender equality in many societies, they failed to produce good results on the distribution of household duties in many Zimbabwean societies as women are still burdened with the responsibility of taking care of the children, the sick and the elderly. Equality in terms of care giving is still a long way to be achieved in Zimbabwe. Men step into care giving roles only when women are unavailable and even then, maintain the dominant culture's ideology that it is women who are the natural care givers (Kaye and Applegate 1990 cited by D'Cruz 2004:15) In this regard, the promotion of women owned businesses enables them to have sufficient income to take care of the family and to meet their basic needs. It is important to note that care giving is a difficult task to perform in situations where there is insufficient income. Therefore, when women are empowered through entrepreneurship, the task becomes easier as they could afford to buy food, clothes, and other commodities, as well as paying for medical expenses. In addition, when women are empowered through entrepreneurship it improves the education of their children, as well as improving their nutrition which reduces infant mortality and maternal mortality.

Secondly, women owned business boost economic growth. Women entrepreneurship plays a critical role in economic growth and development (Mitchelmore and Rowley 2013 cited by Derera *et al* 2014:671). It is generally agreed among many scholars that women entrepreneurship does not only reduce poverty among women, but also boosts the development of their countries. Women owned businesses if properly managed can lead to an increase in Gross Domestic Product (GDP). Gross Domestic Product is defined as the market value of all goods and services produced in the domestic economy during a period of one year, plus income earned locally by the foreigners minus incomes earned abroad by the nationals (Dwived 2004: 462). As women businesses increases, in a country tax revenue also increase since some women's businesses are registered hence, they pay tax. At the same time, their employees also pay tax (Pay As You Earn (PAYE)). By so doing, the economy of the country will be enhanced. Income collected through taxation can be used to pay the salaries of civil servants as well as infrastructural development. All these help to boost the economy of the country.

Thirdly, women owned businesses enable women to be visible in society. The lower status of women mostly stems from their low economic status and subsequent dependence as well as lack of decision making power, hence if women gain economic strength, they gain visibility and voice (Charantimath 2006: 111). Women businesses give women the opportunity of economic independence, which in some cases can help them to acquire political muscles as well as improving their social status. Acquiring economic power in a way paves the way for women to become visible and recognised in their societies.

Impediments to women's entrepreneurship in Zimbabwe

Although women owned businesses are increasing at a faster rate in Zimbabwe, women still face a plethora of challenges which in most cases hamper the growth and success of their businesses. A survey carried out among female owned businesses revealed that the success of female entrepreneurship is hindered by several factors which are discussed below.

Most women often encounter the problem of inadequate capital to start their own businesses or make their businesses viable. Women entrepreneurs have more difficulty than male entrepreneurs to obtain credit (Naude and Havenga 2005: 112). This is exacerbated by the fact that most women lack collateral security which is required by many banks and loan lending agencies. Among the women who were interviewed, 80 percent indicated that they got capital to start up their businesses from personal savings, 10 percent indicated that they were financed with their relatives, 5 percent indicated that they borrowed money from money lending agencies (*chimbadzo*). *Chimbadzo* is a Shona word referring to a business activity whereby people (either individuals or groups) lend money to borrowers and they charge interest rates which range from 15 percent to 30 percent in Zimbabwe. Although this businesses activity is illegal except only for registered companies, some women are partaking in this business and are making reasonable profits. Only 5 percent of women in business indicated that they borrowed their capital from banks. Due to these financial constraints, most women owned businesses in Zimbabwe dominate small enterprises which are in most cases informal.

Some women businesses in Zimbabwe are affected by poor managerial skills. Considering the fact that women entrepreneurs are not a homogenous group in Zimbabwe, some women have low levels of education, while among those with reasonably levels of education, their education has little or nothing to do with business management, for example teachers and nurses. This hampers the growth of their businesses because they lack skills necessary to promote the growth and effectiveness of their businesses. The 2012 report by the OECD council states that the two key differences between male and female entrepreneurs is that women start their enterprises with limited experience and they devote much less time to their businesses than men. Thus, because of lack of managerial skills, most women find it difficult to boost their businesses even in situations where they have adequate funds. People in business require a whole range of training and capacity support (beginning from social skills, like leadership, conflict resolution, negotiation and participation to techno-managerial skills, financial literacy, accountancy, records keeping, business management skills among others (Dash 2012:200)

To some extent, women's household roles affect the performance of business among Zimbabwean women. In most African societies, there is a general perception that women are the ones who must perform household duties such as preparing food for the family, taking care of the children, cleaning, laundry, etc. This is mainly because of gender roles which are deeply embedded in their culture. Many women who were interviewed, about 75 percent, indicated that household duties affect their performance in business. These were mostly women who engage in business activities such as vending and other small enterprises. Most of them indicated that profit from their businesses does not allow them to have maids, hence they perform all the household chores themselves. Some women in this category even take their infants with them when they go to their business activities and this affects their performance as they need to serve their clients and at the same time take care of their infants. This is very common among women who work in salons, vending and cooperatives, though not in all cases. However, about 25 percent of women in business indicated that their business is not affected by household chores. Some indicated that they are helped by maids, while others indicated that their husbands sometimes help them. Others indicated that they manage their time in such a way that it does not affect their business by waking up early in the morning.

Conclusion and Recommendations

There is increasing recognition among many countries, both developed and developing, that female entrepreneurship is a key driver to development. Women in Zimbabwe are partaking in many business activities such as money lending clubs, co-operatives, vending, while others are run their own salons, restaurants, and grocery shops among others. Some, though just a few, are growing their businesses beyond the need for survival and are opening up big firms in clothing industry, construction and mining. Many women entrepreneurs are doing their businesses due to their religious motivation. Women owned businesses are important in countries such as Zimbabwe where the economy is not stable and is leading to the closure of many big firms which also amounts to high unemployment rates and increasing poverty among many people in the country. In this regard, women owned businesses are playing an important role in Zimbabwe as they serve as a poverty reduction strategy through employment creation and increased income at household and national levels. However, although many women in Zimbabwe are participating in business, in some cases the profit obtained is marginal. Most of them face several constraints which hinder the growth and success of their businesses. These challenges include financial constraints which are often caused by lack of access to credit facilities due to lack of collateral security, poor managerial skills, limited time due to household duties among others. Although the government of Zimbabwe signed several protocols and conventions such as the Beijing Platform for Action as well as enforcing several Acts which aims at reducing inequalities and increasing women's participation in business, it has failed to effectively remove the constraints faced by women in business.

The study recommends that the government and other organisations should increase funding for women businesses. Further, faith-based organisations must be supported as they have the potential to empower women in business. Although the government sometimes sets aside funds for women's businesses, it is still not enough to cater for all women entrepreneurs in the whole country, hence there is need for an increment. There must be also short training courses for women entrepreneurs so as to improve their business managerial skills.

References

Abdullah, M.A. and Bakar M.H. *Small and Medium Enterprises in Asian Pacific Countries: Roles and Issues,* New York, Nova Science Publishers, Inc, 2000.

Bauer, J. *The Flight of the Pheonix: Investing in Zimbabwe's Rise from the Ashes during the Colonial Global Debt Crisis,* Berlin, epubli, 2013.

Brown, M. E. *Famine Early Warning Systems and Remote Sensing Data,* Berlin, Springer Science and Business Media, 2008.

Charantimath, P. M. *Entrepreneurship Development and Small Business Enterprise,* New Delhi, Pearson Education, 2006.

Chitando, E. "African Instituted Churches in Southern Africa: Paragons of regional Integration. *African Journal of International Affairs,*" vl,7, Nos 1 and 2, 2004.

Chitando, E. *Singing Culture: A Study of Gospel Music in Zimbabwe*: Uppsala, Nordic Africa Institute, 2002.

Chitando, E. "Deliverance and Sanctified Passports: Prophetic Activities amidst Uncertainty in Harare," in Haram, A.and Yamba, C. B. (eds.), *Dealing with uncertainty in contemporary African lives*.Nordiska African Institute, 2009.

Coughlin, J.H. and Thomas, A. R.*The rise of Women Entrepreneurs: People, Processes and Global Trend*, Westport, Greenwood Publishing Group, 2002.

Chiweza, D. *Out of the Rabble: Ending the Global Economic Crisis by Understanding the Zimbabwean Experience*, Bloomington, iUniverse, 2013.

Chopamba, L. *The Struggle for Economic Support of the Indigenous Women Business in Zimbabwe*, Bloomington , XLIBRIS Corporation, 2010.

Dash, A. in Franz, H. et al. (eds), *Challenge Social Innovation: Potentials for Business, Social Entrepreneurship, Welfare and Civil Society*, New York, Springer, 2012.

Derera E. et al, in Kubacki, K. *Ideas in Marketing: Finding the New and Polishing the Old: Proceedings of the 2013 Academy of Marketing Science*, New York, Springer International Publishing, 2014.

Doxtader, E. and Villa-Vicencio, C. *Through Fire with Water: The Roots of Division and the Potential for Reconciliation in Africa*, Claremont, New Africa Books, 2003.

Dwivedi, D.N. *Managerial Economics, 7 E*, Noida, Vikas Publishing House, 2009.

D'Cruz, P. *Family Care in HIV/AIDS: Exploring Lived Experience*, New Delhi, Sage Publications, 2004.

Europa Publications, Murison, K. (ed), *South of the Sahara 2004*, London, Psychology Press, 2003.

Kanyenze, G. *Beyond the Enclave: Towards a Pro-Poor Inclusive Development Strategy*, Harare, Weaver Press, 2011.

King, D. W. *This Business of Gospel Music: How to make money and achieve success in today's United States, Canada and United Kingdom Gospel Music Industry*, Gospel knowledge Books, 2012.

Lupinacci, A. S. *Women and Business Ownership: Entrepreneurs in Dallas, Taxas, Garland Studies and Entrepreneurship*, New York, Taylor and Francis, 1998.

Markovic, M. R. in Markovic M.R. (ed) *The Perspective of Women's Entrepreneurship in the Age of Globalisation*, Charlotte, IAP, 2007.

Michael, R. *The Gospel Music According to Saint Ralph Michael*, I AM-THAT-I AM publishing company, 2005.

Mboko, S. and Smith-Hunter, A. "Zimbabwe Women Business Owners: Survival Strategies and Implications for Growth," *Journal of Applied Business and Economics*, vol. 11 (2), 2009

Msipah et al, "Entrepreneurial Training Needs Analysis in Small-Scale Artisanal Engineering Business in Zimbabwe: A case study of Mashonaland West Province," *Journal of Sustainable Development in Africa*, Vol.15 (2), 2013.

Munyikwa, H. in Hudson et al (eds), *Peace, Conflict and Identity: Multidisplinary Approaches to research*, Bilbao, University of Deusto, 2009.

Muzvidziwa, V.N. "Cross-Border Trade: A Strategy for Climbing out of Poverty in Masvingo, Zimbabwe," *Zambezia*, XXV (i), 1998.

Naude, W.A and Havenga, J.J.D. in Anderson R.B. et al, "An Overview of African Entrepreneurship and Small Business Research," *The Journal of the Canadian Council for Small Business and Entrepreneurship*, Volume 18 (1), 2005.

Ncube, M. Employment, Unemployment and the Evolution of labour policy in Zimbabwe, *Zambezia*, XXVVII, (ii), 2000.

Permanent Mission of the Republic of Zimbabwe to the United Nations: Statement by H.E. Chitsaka Chipaziwa, Ambassador and Permanent Representative of the Republic of Zimbabwe to the United Nations, on Agenda Item 28: Advancement of Women.

Porter, R. B. et al, *Geographies of Development: An Introduction to Development Studies*, 3rd Edition, Essex, Pearson Education Limited, 2008.

Sachikonye, L. M. in Burgess, J et al *Review of Political Economy*, New York, Routledge, 2006

Sibanda, F. and Maposa, R.S. in Chitando, E. Gunda, M. R and Kugler, J. *Multiplying the Spirit: African Initiated Churches in Zimbabwe*, Bamberg, Bamberg Press, 2014.

Todaro, M.P. and Smith, S.C. *Economic Development*, 11th Edition, Essex, Pearson Education Limited, 2011.

Vossenburg, S. *Women Entrepreneurship Promotion in Developing Countries: What Explains the Gender Gap in Entrepreneurship how to close it?* Maastricht, Maastricht School of Management, 2013.

World Bank Discussion Paper No. 403 in Chao, S. (ed), Washington DC, World Bank Publications.

Zeidan, S. and Bahrami, S. "Women Entrepreneurship in GCC: A framework to Address Challenges and Promote Participation in a Regional Context," *International Journal of Business and Social Science*, Vol. 12 (2)

Zimbabwe Millennium Development Goals, 2004 Progress Report.

Zimbabwe National Statistics Agency (ZIMSTAT), 2012 Report.

http://www.entrepreneurshipafrica.com/business-resources/entrepnews/food-world-supermarket-chain-born-out-of-tuck-shop-savings.html

CHAPTER 4

Postcolonial Zimbabwean Economy
A Theological Hindsight
RICHARD S. MAPOSA

Introduction

ZIMBABWE IS A COUNTRY situated in Southern Africa. In terms of population, as of 1 January 2015, the country was estimated to have 15 804 584 people. Of these people, 49.3% are males and 50.7% are females (Zimbabwe Population, 2015). Zimbabwe is an archetypal postcolonial State whose economy, or, in more concrete terms, political economy is shattered, basically on account of the ripple effects of colonialism. As Leela Gandhi (1998:17) has rightly observed, the ogre of colonialism does not end with the end of colonial occupation itself. Outside the orbit of South Africa, then in 1980, Zimbabwe was regarded as the jewel (gemstone = precious stone) of sub Saharan Africa when it got independence. The country had a hopeful future and no one expected the economy to plunge (Bond, *et al*, 2003). Nevertheless, in order to put Zimbabwe's economic trajectory in its proper picture, three distinctive phases are identified. In his doctoral thesis presented at the University of Zimbabwe, Maposa (2014:169ff) formulated three critical phases that provide a key framework to analyze Zimbabwe's political economy in the postcolonial setting. These are "the hopeful advance," "turbulent swing" and "radical watershed" phases. In general, these phases are critiqued in line with the enduring ideas posited by Edward Wadie Said (1935–2003), the insightful Palestinian-American theoretician of postcolonial studies. In part,

Said, as cited in Dube (2000:68) argued that 'modern imperialism was so global and all-encompassing that nothing virtually escaped it, besides, as I have said, the nineteenth-century contest over empire is continuing today. . ..' We are citing this insight to demonstrate that the non-performance of Zimbabwe's current political economy should be properly understood from what globalization can do to the economies of the Third World countries. The chapter critiques Zimbabwe's postcolonial economy by blending the historical method and theological insights on the level of presentation and interpretation, respectively. Below is an exposition of the key characteristics of the identified phases which mirror the nature of the postcolonial Zimbabwean economy.

'The Hopeful Advance,' 1980-1990

The first phase ushered in a hopeful advance for Zimbabwe which had emerged from the ashes of the *Chimurenga* war (1966-1980). The phase represented the period of progress in the life of the country. The phase was linked to the political euphoria inspired by the principles of a Marxist socialist economy. It must be noted that Mugabe's government was supported by the churches and external donors on economic reconstruction because it was not 'bent on creating a godless society' (Banana, 1996:236). The decade-long phase was hopeful because the country had inherited a worthwhile and promising economy from the colonial period. The new black government was expected to sustain, improve and continue performing the economic renewal due to conditions which prevailed on the ground. For instance, Smith's colonial economy bequeathed relatively good infrastructure, railway system, air services, banking system, trading partners and manpower with technical know-how to the new black-managed economy. Moreover, the economic sanctions which plagued Smith's government between 1965 and 1980 were scrapped by the West since Mugabe's ZANU (PF) government restored international legality and diplomacy. As part of its national policy enunciated in the ZANU (PF) Manifesto (1980), the new government undertook considerable broad-based programmes for national economic reconstruction. It is prudent also to indicate that financial institutions such as the African Development Bank, World Bank and the International Monetary Fund backed up Zimbabwe's road to economic recovery. Evidently, these key factors, among others, created a hopeful dispensation for the reconstruction of the Zimbabwean economy. To bring this new economic roadmap to fruition, the government, churches and NGOs/private sector partnered on community development across the country. For instance, these three players collaborated on the early land re-settlement to redress and address the land imbalances going back to the time of colonial occupation in order to sustain the public programme of *zadza matura* (food security). It is prudent that we provide some details on the linkages between the early land distribution exercise and the national initiatives on food security undertaken during the 'hopeful advance phase under review.

Linking the Economy, *Zadza Matura* and Early land Redistribution

The term, *zadza matura,* refers to the capacity building on food security for people in their communities and the country as a whole. *Zadza matura* further implies that people, especially in the rural areas, must work to ensure that they run away from famine and halt the challenges of persistent malnutrition in view of lack of formal employment. The underlying perception is that people must not suffer from an economic dependency syndrome but to sustain themselves. In fact, the spirit of *zadza matura* was perceived to be part of economic reconstruction which also guided the pastoral praxis of the churches in a new Zimbabwe. The churches themselves were receptive to the national call on food security because they interpreted it as part of the divine mandate to work for the people. The churches saw it well that development was about people, but people had to develop themselves within their situatedness. Let us utilize the example of one key mainline church denomination to demonstrate how the churches were involved in economic reconstruction by supporting the programme of resettlement in Zimbabwe. In November 1981, the United Church of Christ in Zimbabwe (hereafter, UCCZ) owns three mission farms in Chipinge district, namely, Mt Selinda Mission Farm, Chikore Mission Farm and Southdown Mission Farm. The UCCZ divided its large farms into the new mission village where the landless people were resettled. The resettled people were sub divided into work- teams and skills- brigades. These agricultural syndicates enhanced food production as the villagers were given free seeds or seedlings, fertilizers, draught ploughs on the basis of loans, technical advice from agricultural extension workers, among other things. Despite some challenges, it delightful to note that the early resettlement exercise was fairly successful during the 1980s. Again, by using the example of the UCCZ, we see that by the end of 1983, Chikore and Mt Selinda farms were able to feed their two boarding schools, then. These missions had last managed to feed their schools back in 1974. On the whole, it must be underscored that The UCCZ represents the churches in that support the government on the issues of economic development and reconstruction. The Roman Catholic Church, the two Methodist churches, Presbyterian Church, Anglican Church, Salvation Army and Seventh Day Adventists, for instance, also undertook notable resettlement programmes. It is important to note that by 1986, about 162 000 landless peasants, who formerly lived in the unproductive communal lands, were resettled on white-owned commercial farms across the country. In terms of the numbers of black families, 48 000 were resettled by 1991, again, across the country. By 1998, the number of black families rose to 70 000 (Shoko, 2006:4). These people were helped by the government, church and private sector with several inputs such as maize seed, fertilizers, draught ploughs (sometimes even with tractors) and technical logistics that boosted the early agrarian developments. It must be added that the issue of development is not restricted to agriculture, but to other key sectors like public construction of roads, bridges, schools, hospitals, industries, and the like. The significance of these developments was that lives were transformed and the country earned a good international image. Nevertheless, Zimbabwe's economy was injured by the horrors and impact of the *Gukurahundi* destabilization that took place, roughly between 1983 and 1985.

'The Turbulent Swing,' 1990–1999

The turbulent swing era represented a period of socio-economic decline and frustration. The era witnessed the introduction of the liberal market reforms to open up the economy between 1990 and 1999. It also witnessed the introduction of corporate measures and the devaluation of the Zimbabwean dollar by 40%. In addition, there was strict governmental control on all aspects of the economy for much of the 1990s. The key characteristics of the liberal era are outlined below. First, there were government restrictive measures of control that were placed on wages, prices of goods that were worsened by government spending. The net result was on the national fiscal which shrank and degenerated into budget deficits. Second, there were shortages of technical and managerial skills that led to bureaucratic inefficiencies. Third, there was inadequate funding in the State-initiated programmes and projects. The World Bank and IMF were not committed to sponsoring economic projects further in view of the new policies of enshrined in the Economic Structural Adjustment Policies (ESAP) that these US-based funders were enunciating, not only for Zimbabwe, but also for the rest of the Third World countries that were 'crying' for financial aid from the West. The impact of these characteristic features of the economy was great on ordinary people, and even worse under the ESAP, which is discussed in the next section.

Economic Structural Adjustment Programme

The liberal era which dawned in the early 1990s saw the development a new phenomenon of human retrenchment. The ESAP was introduced in 1991 as a broad-based comprehensive national programme financed by the Reserve Bank of Zimbabwe (RBZ) with funding from the African Development Bank (it injected US$4.6 million), World Bank and International Monetary Fund (the western institutions both injected US$125 million). These monies were injected to provide balance of payments in the implementation of ESAP in supporting the liberalized economy. Several people were laid off their jobs to join a large stream of the informal sector. The informal sector ballooned because there was joblessness which created human despondency as there were no alternative official jobs. The families of the retrenched lot were pauperized into wretched poverty due to declining economic performance and rising economic debt burden. Moreover, it must be pointed out that the ailing economy continued to deteriorate due to the growing corruptive and nepotistic tendencies associated with the emerging black elite in postcolonial Zimbabwe. The appalling Willovale Motor scandal of 1989 wherein Mugabe's Senior Cabinet Minister, Maurice Nyagumbo was embroiled and eventually committed suicide bears testimony to this economic cancer. The ESAP was a forced economic measure and Mugabe's government adopted it to experiment with the people so much that the net results were mixed. As it were, many of the national projects for economic reconstruction were halted 'half baked' and some collapsed as mere 'white elephants' across the country. The responses in some quarters of the Zimbabwean population began to raise voice sharply. For example, the works under the umbrella of the Zimbabwe Congress of Trade Unions and University of Zimbabwe students started strong activism against the insensitivity of the government for not redressing the national economy. The University of Zimbabwe students demonstrated and clashed with the police in three consecutive years: 1990, 1991 and 1992 to express their discontentment with the government. The students were soon supported by the workers and trade unionists. For instance, in 1994 and 1996, there were widespread industrial unrests perpetrated by the civil servants like nurses, teachers and junior doctors over salaries that were eroded by the poor economy. A year later, in 1997, the national strike was joined by the war veterans. Accordingly, Mugabe's government panicked at the involvement of the war veterans who were at the heart of prosecuting the second *Chimurenga* in the 1970s. This is the context under which the unplanned war veterans' gratuities were paid in 1997. Although the money was not budgeted for, the war veterans were each paid gratuities to the tune of Z$50 000, 00 and pensions each. The process was political expediency, but it strained the economy further to the extent that economic growth, employment opportunities, wages and social services contracted markedly. Worse, inflation began to balloon as deficit remained well above the target in view of Zimbabwe's participation in the Democratic Republic of Congo conflict in the late 1990s. The national fiscal was overburdened because the military involvement was costly. As a result, Zimbabwe's military participation, though pragmatic in terms of foreign policy justification, rendered the helpless people to literally 'vote with their feet' (Gaidzanwa, 1999). This is how the economy of the liberal era negatively imprinted on many of Zimbabwe's citizens.

'The Radical Watershed,' 2000–2015

The period from 2000 been a long era of crisis and justifiably regarded as radical in as much as it constitutes a momentous and ground-breaking pendulum in the history of Zimbabwe as a postcolonial State. The era is characterized by political horror and economic collapse. Peter Lewis (1996) posits that Zimbabwe's tumultuous situation in this radical era provides the model where predatory rule reigns. A predatory rule is represented by a regime that sustains itself through coercion and material inducement and tends to discredit the foundations of the institutions of the State. The essence of predatory rule is that the ruling group of people is preoccupied with its own survival through strategies like conspiracies, counter-conspiracies, terrorism, counter-terrorism, purges and counter- purges, among others.

The radical era emerged in the backdrop of considerable opposition to President Mugabe's government. There was the formation of the Movement for democratic Change party in 1999 under the leadership of Morgan Tsvangirai. The MDC plunged into the turbulent political topography when it influenced the 'No' vote to the Constitutional referendum in February 2000. The referendum was handily defeated and Mugabe's government was embarrassed. It must be underscored that the whole gamut of Zimbabwe's existence was soon transformed in quite fundamental ways that either facilitated to restore the lost heritage on account of colonialism or aroused fears from certain international quarters. This later perspective provides the backdrop of the imposition of sanctions. These circumstances are helpful to explain why the Zimbabwean economy continues to be in conundrum in the postcolonial milieu, 'Inside Third *Chimurenga*' (Sibanda and Maposa, 2014). I also wish to state that the economic conundrum under review in the new millennium manifests, in broad terms, what is generally described as the 'Zimbabwe Crisis'. Let us briefly highlight the terrains of the 'Zimbabwe crisis' in the light of the national economy that Zimbabweanshavein contradiction to what Zimbabweans want. In fact, it is perceptively declared that the Zimbabwe *we have* is diametrically poles apart from the kind of Zimbabwe *we want*. This is the gamut of the thesis that lies behind the narration of the 'Zimbabwe crisis' which is intelligible enough to explain the nature of the political economy in Zimbabwe, today.

'Zimbabwe Crisis' and the Economy

Today, Zimbabwe is a country experiencing a deep crisis. The 'Zimbabwe crisis' started to show its ugly face in the mid-1990s. The manifestations were mass unemployment, prostitution, brain drain, electricity power cuts, inflation, shortage of consumer goods, family breakdown, street kids and sanctions. As Hammar, *et al* (2003:4) have shown, following the loss of a national referendum on a Draft Constitution in February 2000, the ZANU (PF) government undertook a land reform programme, code-named, *Third Chimurenga*. The land reform programme caused shockwaves internationally because it was perceived as unsystematic (Eyre, 2001). Its mechanics were violent. Most white farmers were literally dragged out of their farms, their property burnt and without compensation (Bond, *et al*, 2002). Following the spiral of violence, Zimbabwe was isolated diplomatically and the economy melted down with rapidity. Moreover, the social delivery social sectors like on health and education collapsed (*The Daily News*, 2002). The high level of lawlessness worsened all this, as institutions such as the police, army and prison services came to support the ZANU (PF) government (Raftopoulos, *et al*, 2004: ix). The living standards of many Zimbabweans declined. The Zimbabwean crisis reached its peak following the much-disputed Presidential election of March 2008. Thereafter, the political terrain of the country plunged into the Machiavellian law of the jungle. The two arch rivals, the ZANU (PF) party's Robert Mugabe and MDC party's Morgan Tsvangirai wrestled for the support of the people, largely because the Tsvangirai's MDC party had got 47.9% as against the ZANU (PF)'s 43.2% of the national vote. This result prompted for a re-run of the elections in July 2008 but Tsvangirai boycotted that election due to unprecedented violence that mirrored the proverbial fight of elephants whereby the grass suffers. We are citing this sad chapter of the political history of Zimbabwe to demonstrate the fact that the economy continued to collapse due to the political predicament. For instance, the Southern African Development Community and international communities were quite skeptical about the results of the re-run where President Mugabe was the sole candidate. This explains why the EU and US reacted by increasing the economic embargo on Zimbabwe in view of the fact that the civil society was politicized and militarized. From a theological perspective, the new predatory rule reflected the triumph of State theology, supporting the ZANU (PF) political *status quo*, at the expense of prophetic theology, which was silenced ruefully.

It is out of the background described above that the study is justified in engaging a theological reflection on the postcolonial economy and also analyses certain Christian responses or reactions in the backdrop of crisis in Zimbabwe. In general, the Christian responses took different forms and patterns. The complication could be accounted for by the fact that Christians reacted, sometimes as individuals or denominations. The latter form was usually expressed through the high echelons of the church leadership. Nevertheless, as the study envisions, those responses whether exhibited by individuals or denomination as a whole, reveal a surging theology of re-construction. As Chitando (2009) has shown, Reconstruction theology suits battered economies, shattered social systems and unstable political systems. The study perceives re-construction theology as a hermeneutical tool and as part of a theological mutation seeking the renewal of churches so that they may brave themselves to tackle the crisis towards building new communities in Africa. From the ruins of the 'failed States' in Africa, the best we can tell is that the task(s) of the Christian churches as guided by the new panorama of re-construction theology. Again, as cited in Chitando (2009:103) Mugambi specifically asserted that re-construction theology:

> Should be reconstructive rather than destructive, inclusive rather than exclusive, proactive rather than reactive, complementary rather than competitive, integrative rather than disintegrative, people-centred rather than institution-centred, deed-oriented rather than word-oriented, participatory rather than autocratic, regenerative rather than degenerative, cooperative rather than confrontational, consultative rather than impositional'.

In the next section, we start by highlighting the land reform movement as a fundamental aspect of the radical watershed era in postcolonial Zimbabwe.

The Land Reform Programme and the Economy

The agrarian reform followed the failure of the Constitutional Referendum in February 2000. Mugabe's government was irritated because it attributed the failure of the referendum to white pressure. Yet, the white community accounted for less than 1% of the entire population but owned about 70% of the arable land (Moyana, 2000; Maposa, 2012). This is the historical context under which ZANU (PF) party government instructed the *povo* (peasants) to invade and compulsorily acquire the white-owned commercial farms. The soldiers, police and militias were instructed not to stop the landless black invaders. Today, much of the commercial land previously in white farmers is now in the hands of *varimi vatsva* (black farmers). Far from being political expediency, President Mugabe rightfully acclaimed that the 'economy is land and land is the economy' because the radical land ownership paradigm constitutes the fountain for genuine Zimbabwean empowerment and black identity-with-pride. This hindsight, in part, captures the quintessence behind the notions of 'Proudly Zimbabwean'. By April 2001, about 17 000 white commercial farms were seized and occupied by *varimi vatsva* (Eyre, 2001).

After 2005, economy was structured to follow the principles of a command economy which called for 'extraordinary measures for extraordinary challenges' that had emerged out of extra ordinary circumstances (Gono, 2008:130). Dr. Gideon Gono, who was the Reserve Governor of Zimbabwe (RBZ) between 2004 and 2014, advocated for the implementation of austere fiscal policies to deal with the casino economic environment at the height of the crisis that engulfed Zimbabwe for much of the revolutionary era. The justification was that Mugabe's government (any government worldwide, for that matter!) was surrounded by both the internal external threats. Among other issues, the 'casino economy' situation can be exemplified by the value of the Zimbabwe dollar versus US dollar cross rates and also the inflation rates that soared to quite unprecedented levels between March 2000 and March 2008. Let the statistics speak for themselves. First, in terms of cross rate comparative financial figures, for example, in February 2003, US $1.00 matched Z$2 500.00. In February 2004, US1.00 was stretched to match Z$6.500.00 (Miller, et al, 2004: 80). At the height of the financial crisis in 2008, US1.00 was overstretched to match something like Z$1 000 000.00 (one million, in Bearer Cheque form). Second, in terms of the inflation rates, in February 2000, the inflation was at 420% mark. In November 2005, the inflation rate rose to 856%. And a year later in November 2006, inflation rate soared to 1 070%. On the eve of the harmonized national elections of March 2008, the inflation rate had sky-rocketed to a staggering 120 000%. Rightly so, Gono (2008:130) sought to abandon 'textbook economics' and strategically adopted extraordinary measures for extraordinary challenges associated with the deep-seated economic crisis after 2005! The government scrapped the local Zimbabwean dollar and adopted what came to be called, bearer cheques. But, these Bearer cheques were a burden for majority of Zimbabweans. It was burdensome to see people carrying a bag of bearer cheques (money) in order to buy, say a box of matches at the market tuck-shop. It was also burdensome to be yoked to a bag of bearer cheques when trying to use, say, as combi fare or bus fare when travelling. Most Zimbabweans ended up, literally, 'burning' the bearer cheques in exchange of other currencies like the South African Rand, US dollar, Mozambique's Metical and Botswana Pula. Nevertheless, in the end the printed bearer cheques became worthless as they changed value on a daily basis, from one million to one quintillion against the US$1 by 2008. These high fluid rates of inflation are cited to show that the people's shopping basket became smaller and smaller on a daily basis. Fair-minded people argued that the economy was being 'injured' by the economic sanctions that were imposed by the EU, USA and their allies on 24 September 2001 and onwards. The situation was exacerbated by the US Law S494 which was enacted to bring Zimbabwe's economy to its knees. From the inception of the economic sanctions in 2001, Zimbabwe's economy has continued to reel unabated. This is how the national economy plummeted and provides a link to the emergence of Diaspora phenomenon in contemporary Zimbabwe. As much as we can say, the Diaspora trend has a lot to do with the poor performance of the postcolonial Zimbabwean economy. The foregoing point evokes the enduring insights that the Jamaican Marxist historian, Walter Rodney (1942–1980) posited in his classic book, *How Europe Underdeveloped Africa* (1972). In part, Rodney argued that the rich nations in the western hemisphere are today developed because they enslaved millions of blacks from the African continent from the late the 17th to mid 19th centuries to work in various sectors of their economies. The strong and able-bodied slaves worked all the kind of menial works for them. When labour power is removed and alienated, then that particular community is robbed of the growth potential. This is what is obtaining in Zimbabwe today. At the height of the economic crisis, it is widely believed that about 3.5 million Zimbabweans emigrated to such destinies like Botswana, South Africa, UK, US and Australia, among others. Of these Zimbabwean émigrés, about one million are in the UK and the other several hundred thousand in Canada (Miller, *et al*, 2004:80).

The Impact of Operation Murambatsvina on the Economy

The Zimbabwean economy was also impacted upon by Operation *Murambatsvina* (Operation Restore Order). *Murambatsvina* was launched by the government in 2005 as a clean-up campaign of cities, towns and growth points to remove *tsvina* (dirty). The operation started in Harare on 19 May 2005 and spread like veldt fire into a nationwide exercise (The Herald, 2005: 1), where the police, acting like 'hawks', adopted a military-style crackdown to demolish the illegal structures such as vegetable and fruit vending sites, tuck shops, flea markets, as well as unauthorized houses (Sibanda, *et al*, 2008: 74). Besides demolishing the illegal structures, Operation *Murambatsvina* was also accompanied by the confiscation of precious items such as minerals, foodstuff, foreign currency and even fuel which were discovered in the dirty hideouts or illegal structures. Many people wrestled fruitlessly with the police, but the victims were overpowered and made to take part in the destruction of their own 'illegal' business structures before they vacated into the 'deep end'. This is how the accommodation crisis emerged and exacerbated by the high levels of joblessness and social frustration. It is interesting to note that *murambatsvina* also targeted the churches, particularly those that conducted their services under the open space. Such churches include the Apostolic and Zionist movements. Sibanda, Makahamadze and Maposa (2008) observed in their 2008 study how churches were banned from worshipping in the open places as they were accused of polluting the environment and creating a potential health hazard. This is why such churches were told to relocate to safer places.

It must also be mentioned that the so-called dirty places that suffered under *Murambatsvina* were associated with the emerging enterprising tendency known as *chikorokoza* (illegal ways of making ends meet in order to survive). This level of destruction was negative so much that *Murambatsvina* was regarded as *tsunami* due to its negative impact it had on every aspect of human life. People involved in this enterprise are called *makorokoza*. Commodities such as cooking oil, flour, bread, sugar and fuel that had become scarce were got through *chikorokoza* but with the implementation of Operation *Murambatsvina*, the *makorokoza* were forcefully dispersed and 'migrated' to the rural areas. Small-scale businesses such as the production of scotch carts, coffins, farm equipment, among others, were neglected as *makorokoza* were displaced and dispersed by Operation *Murambatsvina* across the country. The people's sources of livelihood were destroyed and it helps to demonstrate how the national economy was ruined by Operation *Murambatsvina*. Evidently, the impact of Operation *Murambatsvina* continues to pester the national economy, in critical forms today.

Summary

The study observed that Zimbabwe stands as a beleaguered postcolonial State in Africa, largely on account of its melted political economy. It was noted that the particular economic collapse which was perpetrated, largely on account of political behaviour provides a defining moment of the present generation in Zimbabwe. Three vital phases connected to the dynamics of the political economy were identified in order to configure how society was embossed from 1980 to date. There were some decisive circumstances which turned Zimbabwe's economy from being the 'bread basket' of southern Africa to become the 'basket case' of the region. As such, some of the principal circumstances, like the ESAP, ill-timed war veterans' gratuities, regional civil conflict, chaotic land agrarian revolution, sanctions, disputed national elections, Diaspora phenomenon and the ZANU (PF) party succession wars, among others, have thrown the country into the 'deep end' of the economic Gordian knot, and the ripple effects are hemorrhaging the economy. This is the peculiar economic context, generally, where people are suffering from cognitive dissonance, is Pentecostal Christianity surging with rapidity to gain secured religious foothold in contemporary Zimbabwe. In the context of this study, the women are powered by faith to move on: working to uplift themselves and transform their families and regenerate society at large.

References

Alexander, J. (2007) "The Historiography of Land in Zimbabwe: Strengths, Silences, and Questions" in: *Safundi: The Journal of South African and American Studies*, Vol. 8(2), pp. 183–198.
Bond, P. and Manyanya, M. (2003) *Zimbabwe's Plunge: Exhausted Nationalism, Neoliberalism, and the Search for Social Justice*, Harare: Weaver Press.
Challenge to the Church: The Kairos Document: Theological Comment on the Political Crisis in South Africa, Gweru: Mambo Press, 1985.
Churches in Manicaland (2006) *The Truth Will Make You Free: A Compendium of Christian Social Teachings*, Mutare: Churches in Manicaland.
Dube, M.W. *Postcolonial Feminist Interpretation of the Bible*, Danvers: Chalice Press, 2000.
Eyre, Banning, *Playing with Fire*, Copenhagen: Freemuse handy-Print, 2001.
Gandhi, L. *Post colonial Theory: A Critical Introduction*, Edinburgh: Edinburgh University Press, 1998.
Gono, G. *Zimbabwe's Casino Economy: Extraordinary Measures for Extraordinary Challenges*, Harare: ZPH Publishers, 2008.
Maposa, R.S. 'Christianity and Development: History of the United Church of Christ in Zimbabwe and the Emergence of Liberation Theology, 1965 – 2005', Unpublished PhD Thesis, University of Zimbabwe, Harare, 2014.
Maposa, R.S. 'Land to the Landless? Theological Reflections on Some Churches to the Land Reform program in Zimbabwe, 2000–2012, in *Africana*, Vol. No. 2012, pp-78–109.
Miller, D.E., Holland, S., Johnson, D. and Fendall, L, *Seeking Peace in Africa: Stories from African Peacemakers*, Pennsylvania: Cascadia Publishing House, 2004.
Rodney, W. *How Europe Underdeveloped Africa*, Dar es Salaam: EAP, 1972.
Sibanda, F. and Maposa, R.S. "Beyond the Third Chimurenga?: Theological Reflections on the Land Reform Programme in Zimbabwe, 2000–2010," *The Journal of Pan African Studies*, Vol. 6(8), 2014.
Sibanda, F., Makahamadze, T. and Maposa, R.S. 'Hawks and Doves: The Impact of Operation Murambatsvina on Johane Marange Apostolic Church in Zimbabwe, *Exchange: Journal of Theological and Missiological Studies*, Vol.37, 2008, pp 68–85
Shoko, T. 'My Bone Shall Rise Again': War Veterans, Spirits and Land Reform in Zimbabwe, African Studies Centre, Leiden: ASC Working Paper, No. 68/2006.
Raftopoulos, B. (2009) "The Crisis in Zimbabwe, 1998–2008," Raftopoulos, B. and Mlambo, A. (eds.) (2009) *Becoming Zimbabwe: A History from the Pre-colonial Period to 2008*, Harare: Weaver Press, pp. 201–232.

The Kairos Document (1985) *Challenges to the Church: A Theological Comment to the Political Crisis in South Africa*, Gweru: Mambo Press.

Gaidzanwa, R. (1999) *Voting with their Feet: A Study of Zimbabwe Doctors and Nurses in the Era of Structural Adjustment Programme*, Uppsala: Nordiska Afrikainstitutet.

Manase, I. (2014) "Representations of post-2000 Zimbabwean Economic Migrancy in Petina Gappah's *An Elegy for Easterly* and Brian Chikwava's *Harare North*," *Journal of Black Studies*, Vol. 45(1), pp. 59–76.

Mlambo, A. and Raftopoulos, B. (2010) "The Regional Dimensions of Zimbabwe's Multi-Layered Crisis: An Analysis," Downloaded from: http//www.iese.ac.mz/lib/publication/proelit/Alois_Mlambo.pdf, Accessed: 11.12.13.

The Herald, July 28, 2005.

The Daily News, 2002.

Zimbabwe Population, http:www.countrymeters.info/en/Zimbabwe, Accessed: 21.05.15 @1031 Hours.

CHAPTER 5

UFIC's 'Victorious Ladies'

Using the 'Anointing' to Re-claim Christian Women's Economic Space in Zimbabwe

MOLLY MANYONGANISE

Introduction

THE INTENTION OF THIS chapter is to examine at how the United Family International Church (UFIC) is encouraging women in the church to re-claim Christian women's economic space. The United International Church is a fairly young Pentecostal church in Zimbabwe. The chapter will not dwell on the historical background of the church since Biri (2012), Manyonganise (2013), Shoko and Chiwara (2013), as well as Chitando, *et al* (2013) have already dealt with this subject. Building on the afore-mentioned writings, the chapter focuses on UFIC's women's economic participation in Zimbabwe. Utilising gender as a tool for analysis, the chapter seeks to explore ways in which UFIC has encouraged women to be economically independent through entrepreneurship. Data for the paper were gathered through structured interviews, informal discussions, observation, as well as listening to sermons delivered within the UFIC. I write the chapter as an insider, being a member of the church myself. I, therefore, have some privilege in that I have the knowledge of some of the teachings of the church on prosperity. A total of five women entrepreneurs were interviewed. I must, however, hasten to say these were lay believers in the church. It was very difficult to get access to the women who hold high ranks in the church as often times requests to get access were not replied to. UFIC is a highly bureaucratic church where access to those in leadership is not easy. As such, I had to rely on the information from those members in business, but who are not necessarily within the leadership ranks of the church in order to establish the worldview of women entrepreneurs in the church. In order to understand the participation of women in UFIC in the economy, there is need to first look at Pentecostal teachings on prosperity in general.

Pentecostalism and the Prosperity Theology

A number of studies have looked at Pentecostalism and its focus on prosperity and substantial research has documented the association between religion and socio-economic attainment (Heaton, James & Oheneba-Sakyi, 2006: 71). It is difficult to discuss Pentecostalism and ignore what has come to be termed as 'Faith gospel', 'claim it-have it gospel', 'gospel of prosperity' or 'prosperity theology'. This chapter adopts the use of 'prosperity theology' because it encompasses a great deal of what Pentecostals teach on prosperity. This style of doing theology is inspired by Christ's acclamation in John 10:10. Robins cited in Asamoah (2013:198) defines prosperity theology as a "Christian religious doctrine that teaches that financial blessing is the will of God for Christians, and that faith, positive speech, and donations to Christian ministries will always increase one's material wealth." It can also be defined as a "theological current that states that, if certain principles are followed, the expiatory work of Christ guarantees, to all who believe, divine healing, the riches of the world, and happiness without suffering" (Saracco cited in Mombi, 2009:33). In this case, the gospel of prosperity teaches that God desires every Christian to be wealthy, and that true faith leads to prosperity (Spinks, 2003:21). As such, wealth is interpreted as a blessing from God, obtained through a spiritual law of positive confession, visualization, and donations (Wilson quoted in Asamoah, 2013:198). Prosperity doctrines of physical healing, material wealth, and salvation are often summarized in a particular understanding of what Jesus accomplished on the cross (Attanasi and Yong, 2012:5). 2 Cor 8:9 which says, "For you know the grace of our Lord Jesus Christ, that though he was rich, yet he became poor, so that by his poverty you might become rich" (RSV) is critical for justifying the prosperity gospel in Pentecostal churches.

The Pentecostal theology of prosperity looks at poverty as a curse from which members need deliverance. From a Pentecostal perspective, the most effective way to get out of poverty is by way of giving/seeding/sowing to the church. Central to this teaching is Lk 6:38 which encourages Christians to give so that they may be given back. Pentecostal churches have provided ritual contexts in which members can be delivered from the curses of the devil such as poverty which is mostly seen as caused by generational curses. Kwabena Asamoah-Gyadu (2006) notes that the African Pentecostal insistence that it is possible to be Christian and be dominated by desires of the flesh and demonic influences has led to the provision of ritual contexts in which people could renounce such stumbling blocks through healing and deliverance in order that they may be empowered to victory in life. Spinks (2003:22) posits that "the intensity of the Pentecostal movement provides an alternative route for breaking out of socio-economic poverty, with charismatic phrases such as "breakthrough" and "victorious" encouraging women to rise above their individual and national struggles."

Pentecostalism and Women

Like any other form of Christianity in Africa in general and Zimbabwe in particular, Pentecostalism attracts women much more than men (Lechner, & Boli, 2005:181). Scholars have come up with different reasons as to why this is the case. While some have posited that Pentecostalism is empowering to women, others have viewed it as ambivalent, that is, as both empowering and disempowering. For example, Browning and Hollingworth cited in Parsitau (2012:209) have pointed out the gender paradox at the heart of global Pentecostalism, whereby it is at once liberating and disempowering for women. In this case, Parsitau (2012:209) notes that while on the one hand many Pentecostal churches affirm the equality of all human beings and seek to liberate women from traditional cultural structures, they also uphold the sanctity of the patriarchal family and refuse to let women take leadership roles. In her study of Zimbabwe, Mapuranga (2013:77) also observed that despite women constituting the majority in Pentecostal churches, men have dominated positions of power and influence. To this end, Lechner and Boli (2005:181) argue that Pentecostalism does not treat women equally with men because patriarchy is alive and well within its circles.

However, some scholars have looked at Pentecostalism as an empowering agent for women in Africa. Some studies on African Pentecostalism are positive about the contribution that Pentecostalism is making towards gender equality and the empowerment of women (Van Klinken, 2013:245). Kalu cited in Van Klinken (2013:245) argues that "the complementarity in the Spirit between men and women. . .could provide an exit from the shackles of patriarchy," though his views are debatable. For example, in a study in Kenya, Parsitau (2012:203) notes that a new wave of women-led Pentecostal and Charismatic churches has been seeking gendered social transformation. In her view, by "focusing on the gospel message of salvation and redemption, they seek to bring about a transformation in women's lives by empowering them both spiritually and materially" (2012:203). Friedmann (2008:11) has argued that, "Pentecostal movements, while demanding, family-oriented, and gender-stratified, seem to present women with greater possibilities for self-determination, social improvement, and individual empowerment. For him, "women's emancipation within Pentecostalism is predominantly practical" (2008:12) and he views Pentecostalism as a "transformative system for socio-economic betterment" (2008:11). One of the interviewees for this chapter, concurred with the above scholarly views as she claimed that

> Pentecostalism encourages women to work. It treats men and women the same because the gospel of prosperity is preached to both men and women (Vimbai Mazarura, 2015).

In the above interview, Mazarura went further and said that Pentecostalism gives women hope and encouragement to face whatever challenge in their lives. Hence, Omenyo (2014:142) argues that one of the appeals of the pentecostal-charismatic movement is its ability to respond to the existential and pragmatic needs faced by modern urban congregations, including domestic and socio-economic problems. In Pentecostal churches, Mwaura (2007:413) notes that women have been able to surmount various odds in their attempt to shape new communities and new personal and collective movements. This is mainly because of the inclusive nature of the churches, as well as their ability to recognize the varied talents and insights of both men and women (2007:413). These observations present Pentecostalism as endorsing the paradox that religion, anywhere in the world, is an agent of oppression and emancipation. Coming back to Zimbabwe, we find that UFIC women are involved in business ventures in a bid to address and redress the way they are marginalised in the Zimbabwean society.

UFIC in Harare

In Zimbabwe, UFIC has become one of the fastest growing Pentecostal churches, attracting thousands and thousands of congregants every Sunday in Harare alone. Emerging during the country's economic crisis (2008), it has attracted people across the socio-economic and political divide, that is, the poor, the rich, politicians and common people alike. According to Win (2013:17) "this challenges the notion that it is mostly the poor that flock to these churches seeking economic miracles. . .." However, when one looks at the seating arrangement in church, one finds that the congregants are grouped according to the way they give in church. Win (2013:17) in her study of Pentecostalism in Zimbabwe, notes very well that there is a visible divide between where the richer go and where the poorer ones go. In UFIC, there is a concept that was introduced of "partnering with the 'Man of God.'" In this concept, every member of the church is encouraged to pay a certain amount to church as form of partnership. This is over and above the offerings and tithes that are given by members. The partnership money has largely influenced how members in the church are categorized. The members are put into six categories namely: Star which is a group of those that have pledged to give US1000 dollars or more every month; Platinum, a group of those that are able to give US500 dollars or more per month; Gold which is made up of those that give US100 dollars or more every month; Silver, a group of the people that give US50 dollars or more; Bronze which is made up of those that give US10 dollars or more per month and then a group which is referred to as 'Any other' which comprises those that give any amount from a dollar to nine dollars. It is, however, difficult to ascertain the exact numbers of people in these categories, suffice to say the majority of the people appear to be in the 'Any other' group. In Marxist analysis, the poor get poorer, and the rich get richer on a daily basis.

In church, those that give large amounts in partnership are provided with the front seats and are regarded as the 'Very Important Persons' (VIPs). This, according to the church, means that they seat close to the 'anointing' and have easy access to the 'Man of God'. Those that do not have the money are relegated to the periphery or the margins and it takes a 'miracle' for them to access the centre. VIPs are noticeable by their badges which are inscribed 'VIP' for easy identification and their cars have got stickers to the same effect. The 'VIPs', however, constitute the minority in church. While both men and women who cannot give large amounts of money are relegated to the margins, it is women who suffer more by the mere fact that they constitute the majority in the church and also because women in Zimbabwe have traditionally been disadvantaged economically because of patriarchy. In such cases, it becomes important to critique these salient forms of women marginalization that are manifest within Pentecostal churches in general and UFIC in particular.

Though the church has categorized its people into different classes, it has encouraged them to work so that they are able to fend for both their families and the church. Through entrepreneurship, members are assured of upward mobility from lower classes. The various teachings of the church have given birth to both men and women entrepreneurs. In the next section, I focus on women entrepreneurs in UFIC.

Women Entrepreneurs in the UFIC

In UFIC, there is a women's ministry which is led by Ruth Makandiwa, the wife of Emmanuel Makandiwa. These women are put into different groups, namely, the married, widows, the elderly, single mothers and girls. All these women are dubbed "Victorious Ladies," insinuating that the women can rise above any socio-economic challenge in their lives. The women are always taught that they are victors in the home, at work and in business.

UFIC is endowed with a number of women entrepreneurs. As alluded to earlier, some of these women are within the rank and file of the church's leadership. For example, the wife to the founder of the church, 'Prophetess' Ruth Makandiwa is, among other businesses, involved in the clothing retail industry. A stroll within the Central Business District of Harare takes one to registered clothing shops called 'Perceptions'. One of these shops is located along George Silundika Avenue between First and Second Streets. This shop sells quality clothes for both men and women. The second shop in town is located at the Main Post Office and this one sells clothes that are not very expensive. At the Main Post Office, there are several UFIC women who have ventured into the cell phone business. Some of these women are partnering women from other churches. Throughout the CBD, there are UFIC members who are involved in vending and they are easily identifiable by their wrist bands. More often, this has led other members of the church to buy from them since they belong to the same church. One hears members saying *"regai nditengere mwana wemuporofita"* (let me buy from the prophet's child). This very well is in line with the church's teachings that members should support each other's businesses. In this case, the church not only becomes a place of worship, but also of networking for economic empowerment. At UFIC, members advertise their businesses with so much ease as flyers are left on car bonnets, even when the church service is ongoing. According to Win (2013:17) "Pentecostal churches provide access to networks of richer business people thereby opening up even more vistas for prosperity and consumerism." The researcher observed that before the preaching of the Word, wares are sold to congregants, but with the instruction that only authorized vending is permitted. On asking who was authorized to sell products in church, it became clear that apart from the church paraphernalia, the mother and mother-in-law to the founder of the church are the only ones who have that authority. In this case, they sell a range of products such as peanut butter, dried and cooked nuts, roasted fish and fruits among other things. For them, the church becomes a ready market which is often told not to go and buy from 'unsaved' people but must rather promote the women who gave birth to the 'Prophet' and 'Prophetess'.

There is also the need to understand the involvement of women in entrepreneurship in UFIC in the wider context of the doctrine of seeding that is taught in the UFIC. Twice a year, congregants are implored to seed into the life of the 'man' and 'woman' of God. The two days are referred to as 'blessed days'. This in other churches like the Apostolic Faith Mission (AFM) is what is referred to as 'appreciation of the man or woman of God'. Makandiwa, being a former AFM member, might have borrowed this concept from his former church but chose to rename the practice. During this time, congregants are expected to give to the founders of the church both in cash or kind. One rich individuals has given as much as US 28 000 dollars. Others give their cars and houses. In her study of ZAOGA and UFIC, Biri (2012:8) notes that terms such as 'seeding and 'sowing' have become very popular. She argues that "seeding takes various forms, funding church activities and giving to the 'man of God', who is usually the founder of the church. . .." It is generally believed that seeding in these people will bring wealth to the giver. As such, women are expected to contribute through the various groups in the church, that is, the women's ministry, cell groups, zones, departments in which they serve, families and as individuals. For one to be able to contribute to all these groups, one needs a strong financial base. Thus, women have been encouraged to sell various commodities, so that apart from having enough for their families, they are also able to support the 'work of God'.

It seems that the basic teachings in UFIC on prosperity have given the women in the church the courage to earn for themselves. For, example, Ruth Makandiwa (often referred to as 'mother', 'Mama' or 'prophetess') has been presented in church as the model of a wife or woman who should be emulated. Among other characteristics, congregants have been told of how she is enterprising and women in the church who desire to be successful are told to copy the way she does her things. More often, one hears the women in the church saying "*chishuwo changu ndechekuti ndifanane naAmai*" (my desire is to be like mother); often women leaders in the church exclaim that '*amai vedu vanoshanda, havangomiriri kupiwa mari nababa*' (our mother works, she does not wait to be given money by father). Anyone who exhibits a character that is not like that of A*mai* (Mother) is taken not to belong to the UFIC family. This elevation of the wife of the founder has had both positive and negative impact. Positively, it has encouraged women to be proactive in the quest for economic independence. Negatively, it has led women in the church to sacralise her person to the extent that some women in the church cannot envisage buying clothes in any other shop when 'their own mother' is selling the same. The very idea of perceiving her as having a certain kind of 'anointing' because of her closeness to the 'Prophet' has led many to think that they will get that anointing once they get hold of something that has been touched by the 'Prophetess'. This gives her a competitive advantage over other businesswomen in the church who are seen as not carrying the same 'anointing'. This is a fact which is not considered when people give testimonies of how the woman church leader's businesses are successful. Thus, Soothill (2014:211) argues that "the prominence of pastor's wives makes women central figures in Pentecostal and Charismatic churches but also reaffirms the importance of the conjugal relationship to women's social and spiritual status."

Women who were interviewed for this study pointed to the deployment of biblical texts in the church's teachings on business as one of the pillars that has encouraged them to start their businesses no matter how small. Parsitau (2012:219) has noted that "Pentecostal converts seek to shift their mentality from victims to empowered persons who are able to transform their lives using spiritual resources and empowering discourses from biblical sources." In one of the Tuesday services, (which was being beamed on Christ TV, a satellite station owned by UFIC), 'Prophet' Emmanuel Makandiwa taught the congregants that it is the word that should be central when one wants to start a business. Hence, one should not give excuses about not having capital to start with. In this particular instance, he quoted John 3:16 which says " For God so loved the world that he gave his only Son, that whoever believes in him should not perish but have eternal life." He took the verse to reflect how God aids the congregants to start a business. For example, this text was divided into parts. "For God so loved the world" was equated to the vision for business that one receives from God; "that he gave his only son (Jesus)" was equated to the capital for the business that God gives the believer; "that whosoever" is likened to the customers; "believe in Jesus" is equated to the product being sold by the believer; "may have eternal life" is seen as the profit. This deployment of biblical texts to issues that are otherwise considered to be secular has encouraged the women to sell anything that can bring them some profit. For Kalu (2009:14), this is important especially for women because they are empowered to engage the modern economic space and technologies, to operate with optimism that God is with them in the market place, to reject defeat from economic failures from any source. Quite a number of women have received financial assistance from the church to start their businesses.

Another biblical text that has been used in the church to encourage women to be business minded is Proverbs 31. Interviewees concurred that during women's meetings they are taught to be like the woman of Proverbs 31. Mercy Marandure, who buys and sells clothes under the banner of Lendrick fashions says that

> Having been in a Pentecostal church has helped me in my business. Since childhood, I have heard preachers saying that God blesses what we do with our hands and that a woman ought always to work and do business to become a victorious woman of Proverbs (Mercy Marandure, 2015).

According to Frahm-Arp (2014:157), the Proverbs 31 passage "promotes the idea of women working and earning well to support their families and fits well into the 'prosperity theology'. . .." The text projects a woman who is in control of the economic well-being of her family and whose husband gets respected in the public spaces because of her industrious deeds. However, the problem with a lay reading of the text is that it is blind to the gender innuendos that are so glaring. Masenya (2011:94) is of the view that the text is both empowering and disempowering for women. She argues that the "patriarchal order remains entrenched, though subverted by a powerful woman whose many activities are foregrounded." Furthermore, from Masenya's perspective, "the image of a very rich woman with high quality servants can never serve as a model in our [societies]" (2011:94) She, therefore, warns theologians, preachers and the laity alike to be "cautious of not indiscriminately applying elitist texts to poor (women) Bible readers" (2011:94–95).

Other biblical texts which are used in UFIC to justify economic participation highlighted by interviewees are Malachi 3:7–11, 2 Chronicles 20:35, Deut 8:18, Mtt 25:14–30 and Lk 8:2–4. An in-depth discussion on the texts is beyond the scope of the study. It is, however, important to note that Lk 8:2–4 has been critical for women's economic empowerment because it records women who supported Jesus' work out of their own financial resources.

The women also claim that they have been taught business ethics by the UFIC founder. For example, Edith Manjengwa who owns Frank's Fast Foods in Harare's CBD and co-director of Veslag Engineering, a company which deals in irrigation equipment which she owns together with her husband says

> I have been taught about formalizing my business in every aspect, that is, registrations and even paying taxes. I have been taught not to do criminal transactions and to be faithful and say the truth in all my operations (Edith Manjengwa, 2015).

In the same vein, Mercy Marandure says

> The Prophet has taught us to do business God's way where the business has to be registered, pays tax as well as paying tithes as it is a separate entity which needs the hand of God to prosper. We have also been taught not to partner with wicked people in business as God will fight against us. We have been taught to run our businesses the supernatural way (Mercy Marandure, 2015).

Similarly, Vimbai Mazarura who runs a hair saloon called 'Lady Star' in Mabvuku (a high density suburb in Harare) and a canteen called 'Mother Canteen and Take-aways' says she has been taught to run her businesses in a spiritual way (Vimbai Mazarura, 2015). Furthermore, Mercy Marandure says that the Prophet has taught them not to borrow to start a business but to sell what they have in their houses and start from humble beginnings. This could be a way of protecting members from debt. However, it could also be in line with the Pentecostal teaching that members should always be lenders and not borrowers. Prophet Makandiwa is always on record telling his congregants that a borrower is a slave to the lender, as indicated in Prov 22:7.

Interesting to note during the interviews was how members sacralise the person of the founder and the various icons that they are given to use. The women believe that the 'spiritual declarations that are made by the 'Man of God' always ensure that their businesses succeed. Some of the declarations are 'You will make money'; 'Your business shall prosper'; 'You shall not lack'. Apart from the declarations, members receive oil which is referred to as 'anointing oil'. Members of the church have given it a Shona name '*gonan'ombe,*' a term which refers to the oil that is used by indigenous sacred practitioners. Almost all the interviewees alluded to the fact that they trust in the prayers, declarations and the anointing oil which they receive from the church for the success of their businesses. One of them said " as a member, I have received prayers, declarations and anointing oil which have seen me standing in business (Mercy Marandure, 2015) while Vimbai Mazarura claims that the 'Man of God' provides spiritual covering for her business, thereby protecting it from the devil who desires to destroy it. In Cephas Omenyo's opinion, "the belief is that anointing oils, prophetic prayers...complements if not alleviates the practical responsibility of working hard to achieve the desired prosperity in life" (2014:146). Biri (2012) sees in this practice continuities with African Traditional Religions. The only difference may be that the icons are packaged in a more sophisticated way than those in ATRs. Shoko and Chiwara (2013) have given different areas where Emmanuel Makandiwa and the traditional *n'anga* are common and the use of oil is one of them. In UFIC, it is important to note how reference is made not always to the power of God or of the Holy Spirit, but to the 'Man of God'. God becomes the 'God of the Prophet'. During informal discussions, women constantly made this statement '*Nemuporifita zvinoita chete. Ringarambe nepai business nemuporofita wemhando yaPapa?*' (With the prophet everything will be well. How can a business fail with a prophet of Papa's kind?) Thus, apart from the anointing oil for success, members also believe that wrist bands, posters, stickers and other paraphernalia carries the anointing of the prophet which ensures that customers are attracted to the business, as well as to wade off evil generational spirits that may want to fight against one's economic success. In Vimbai Mazarura's saloon, one finds posters with the Prophet and his wife on the wall and all the women workers had wrist bands bearing different messages. The Prophet is, therefore, seen as having the spiritual capacity to avail economic opportunities for his congregants, with women constituting the majority.

Challenges of Women Entrepreneurs in UFIC

While women in UFIC have been encouraged to engage in business, they still face a myriad of challenges. Patriarchy still remains a thorn in the flesh for women entrepreneurs in UFIC. Van Klinken (2013:246) notes that "in different strands of Pentecostal Christianity and in different African contexts, there will definitely be different theological and gender ideological emphases that affect the place and space for women and the configuration of gender relations." The founder of the church seems to be aware of how men within the church (who are products of a patriarchal society) may respond in the face of wives/women who are economically independent. In one of his teachings he said:

> *Unoguma wave chikorobho kusakaraso. Kunzwa vanhu vachiti "ah akadzidza uyu," kutiakadzidza uyu, uri pasi pegambutsu size 14, wakatsikwa bedzi. Unodhirenwa expertisedzese kupera, kubva nechirungu chekuchikoro chinopera kusvika wave kutauranyaudzosingwi vanhu vakati, "a!" wagadziriswa mumarriage nevarume vanotya kudhominetwa. Vanoda madzimai asingashande. Kuthretenwa nekaidea kadiki dikikamhamha wakutothreteneka. "Wakuda kunditonga pano, wakuda kunditonga pano." Babanguwe. Madzimai evamwe ari kutyaira ndege uko, wenyu makangotsikiriramuchifa nenzara* (You end up being a swab, hearing people saying "ah! she is educated that this one is educated, you will be under size 14 gumboots, being suppressed. All expertise is drained from you, including the English language from school until you begin to speak using (Shona) ideophones and people will say ah! Having been sorted in marriage by husbands who are afraid of being dominated, who want wives who do not work, who are threatened by a very small idea from the wife. "You want to control me You want to control me." My Father! (Goodness me!) Others' wives are pilots there, while you suppress your wife, yet you are dying of hunger).

That women were in agreement with the prophet was evident by the way they ululated. After the sermon, informal discussions with various women in church showed that most men, though being members of the church, felt really threatened by women who are economically independent. They also felt that the messages of the Prophet on women economic empowerment were ambivalent because while he has taught that women should be enterprising, he has also taught that as wives they should continue to submit to their husbands. More often, their husbands have capitalized on this, with some of them withdrawing financial support from the family. The women are then left to fend for the family. To this end, Van Klinken (2013:245) notes that the Pentecostal gender discourse embraces traditional Christian notions of gender that are embedded in patriarchal lines of thought. He further argues that the Pentecostal notions of women empowerment coupled with the teachings on wives submitting to their husbands makes the whole discourse on gender equality complex within Pentecostal circles. Prophet Emmanuel Makandiwa often preaches that the reason why women go to work or engage in money-making enterprises is because men are failing to fulfill their God-given duty of being the providers of their families. He argues that there is no need for a wife to go to work if the husband can provide enough for the family. Thus, listening to these teachings, one finds various ambiguities.

Apart from issues of patriarchy, the women lamented the deteriorating economy as another major challenge they were facing in their businesses. They highlighted that people in Zimbabwe no longer had enough disposable income to spend. The continued closure of industries in Zimbabwe had led to many getting unemployed, therefore, the customer base for the UFIC women was also shrinking. In other words, the business environment for these women had become very harsh. Moreso, some of the women interviewed pointed out the lack of business training as one of the major impediments to an otherwise would-be success stories in business. They at times lost a lot of money when they tried out unproven business formulas. From their perspective, training would go a long way in ensuring that they would stick strictly to sound business management strategies.

Conclusion

The discussion above sought to bring out ways in which Pentecostalism enables women to actively participate in Zimbabwe's economic arena. Using UFIC as a case study, the chapter established that women in the church are encouraged to start their own businesses, no matter how small. At the time of writing, a number were in hairdressing, buying and selling, food industry among others. This, to a large extent, was seen as empowering to women. In order to reinforce this point, the study showed how biblical texts were deployed to encourage women to be economically independent. What can be concluded from the above discussion is that UFIC through its teachings has tried to empower women economically. All the interviewees as shown above are of the view that UFIC has provided them with the platform on which to mould their economic lives through the various means discussed, that is, teachings, prayers, declarations, anointing oil among others. Pentecostal Christianity, therefore, provides the innovative panorama of economic change in Zimbabwe. However, the emphasis of UFIC on spiritual matters and its presumed abilities to mitigate economic problems, acts both as a blessing and curse for Zimbabweans. Despite the assertions of bringing emancipation and deliverance to the marginalised women, some people remain in the shackles of poverty. For instance, the classification within UFIC deprives adherents of the ability to critically question issues affecting their sociological profiles in mainstream society. It is also noticeable that the church's subscription to the patriarchal model of gender relations continues to impede women's financial independence. The church, therefore, needs to revisit its stance on gender relations in ways that ensure that women do not continue to be subservient to men, irrespective of their economic status. The church may also need to locate its teachings within the broader context of a deteriorating economy, as well as providing business training sessions for women in business.

References

Asamoah, M.K. 2013.'Penteco/Charismatic Worldview of Prosperity Theology'.*African Educational Research Journal*, Vol. 1(3), pp198–208.

Asamoah-Gyadu, K. 2006. 'African Pentecostal/Charismatic Christianity: An Overview'. *Category: Themed*, Issue 8.

Attanasi, K, 2012. The Plurality of Prosperity Theology and Pentecostalisms'.In Attanasi, K. & Yong, A. (eds.), *Pentecostalism and Prosperity*. New York: Palgrave MacMillan, pp1–19.

Biri, K. 2012. 'The Silent Echoing Voice: Aspects of Zimbabwean Pentecostalism and the Quest for Power, Healing and Miracles.' *Studia, Historiae Ecclesiasticae Supplement*, Vol. 38, 37–55.

Chitando, E., Manyonganise, M. and Mlambo, O. 2013. 'Young, Male and Polished: Masculinities, Generational Shifts and Pentecostal Prophets in Zimbabwe'. In Chitando, E., Gunda, R.M. & Kugler, J. (eds.) *Prophets, Profits and the Bible in Zimbabwe*. Bamberg: University of Bamberg Press.

Frahm-Arp, M. 2014.'African Pentecostalism and Gender Roles'.In Clarke, C.R. (ed.) *Pentecostal Theology in Africa*. Eugene: Wipf and Stock Publishers.

Friedmann, J.L. 2008.'Liberating Domesticity: Women and the Home in Orthodox Judaism and Latin American Pentecostalism'.*Journal of Religion and Society*, Vol. 10, pp2–16.

Heaton, T., James, S. & Oheneba-Sakyi, Y. 2009. 'Religion and Socio-economic Attainment in Ghana,' *Review of Religious Research*, Vol. 51(1), pp71–86.

Kalu, O. U. 2009. 'A Discursive Interpretation of African Pentecostalism'.*Fides et Historia* 41(1), pp71–90.

Lechner, F.J., & Boli, J. 2005. *World Culture: Origins and Consequences*. Oxford: Blackwell Publishing.

Manjengwa, E. 2015.[Personal Interview], 12 April, Harare.

Manyonganise, M. 2013. 'Pentecostals Responding to Gender-based Violence: The Case of the United Family International Church in Harare'. In Chitando, E. and Chirongoma, S. (eds.) *Justice Not Silence: Churches Facing Sexual and Gender-based Violence*. Stellenbosch: EFSA.

Mapuranga, T.P. 2013. 'Bargaining with Patriarchy? Women Pentecostal Leaders in Zimbabwe'.*Fieldwork in Religion*, Vol. 8, No.1, pp74–91.

Marandure, M. 2015. [Personal Interview], 13 April, Harare.

Masenya, M. 2011. The Woman of Worth in Proverbs 31:10–31: Reread through a Bosadi (Womanhood lens) at http://ghfe.org/wp-content/uploads/2013/02/gbfe-jahrbuch-2011-masenya) accessed on 15 April 2015.

Mazarura, V. 2015.[Personal Interview], 10 April, Harare.

Mombi, G. 2009. 'Impact of the Prosperity Gospel in the Assemblies of God Churches of Papua New Guinea'.*Melanesian Journal of Theology*, Vol. 25, No.1, pp32–58.

Mwaura, P.N. 2007. 'Gender and Power in African Christianity: African Instituted Churches and Pentecostal Churches,' in Kalu, O.U. (ed.) *African Christianity: An African Story*. New Jersey: Africa World Press, pp359–388.

Omenyo, C.N. 2014.'African Pentecostalism'. In Robeck, C.M. & Yong, A. (ed.), *The Cambridge Companion to Pentecostalism*. USA: Cambridge University Press.

Parsitau, D. 2012. 'Agents of Gendered Change: Empowerment, Salvation and Gendered Transformation in Urban Kenya'. In Freeman, D. (ed.) *Pentecostalism and Development: Churches, NGOs and Social Change in Africa*. New York: Palgrave Macmillan, pp203–221.

Shoko, T. & Chiwara, A. 2013. 'The Prophetic Figure in Zimbabwean Religions: A Comparative Analysis of Prophet Makandiwa of the United Family International Church (UFIC) and the N'anga in African Traditional Religion. In Chitando, E., Gunda, R.M. & Kugler, J. (eds.), *Prophets, Profits and the Bible in Zimbabwe*. Bamberg: University of Bamberg Press.

Soothill, J. 2014. 'Gender and Pentecostalism in Africa'. In Lindhardt, L. (ed.) *Pentecostalism in Africa: Presence and Impact of Pneumatic Christianity in Post-Colonial Society*. Leiden: Brill Academic Publishers, pp191–219.

Spinks, C. 2003. 'Panacea or Painkiller? The Impact of Pentecostal Christianity on Women in Africa'.*Annual Journal of Women for Women International*, Vol.1, No.1, pp20–25.

Van Klinken, A. 2013. 'God's World is not an Animal Farm- or Is It? The Catachrestic Translation of Gender Equality in African Pentecostalism'.*Religion and Gender*, Vol. 3, No.2, pp240–258.

CHAPTER 6

Faith-Driven Business Ladies
Christ Embassy Women Entrepreneurs in Harare

FUNGAI CHIRONGOMA

Introduction

CHRISTIAN DOCTRINE TEACHES WOMEN to be active. This has been the core of Ladies Meetings (*China*). Proverbs 31:10–31 continues to be the most cited verse for an ideal woman who is submissive to her husband, as well as a woman of valour who provides for her family. In this chapter l argue that religion is working as a source of inspiration for women to engage in business activities. Faith is the motivator and the source of power for women to be engrossed in business activities. The chapter focuses on women in Christ Embassy Church, in particular, praying, fasting and biblical interpretations based on faith motivate them. Pastors' teachings, particularly the literature and inspirational messages of the founder Chris Oyakhilome, are also faith-based sources of motivation for women to engage in business. Despite the challenges that women face, faith gives them confidence and conviction of success in business.

The economic sector has been a male domain because of a general division of labour which has reserved the public sphere for men and the private sphere for women. Women who have ventured in business activities have been stereotyped as they have been regarded as deviating from the norm. Patriarchy idealizes men as breadwinners in the family, thus women have been denied access to most means of generating income. It is not until recently that women have begun engaging in business activities, both small scale and large scale. Pentecostal women are not an exception, their involvement in business is contributing immensely in helping sustain homes in the face of economic crisis in Zimbabwe. A number of factors have inspired Pentecostal women to engage in business activities. However, key among those factors is faith. Faith has worked as a source of inspiration for women to engage in business. This chapter will focus on how faith is inspiring women in Christ Embassy Church to be entrepreneurs. Biblical interpretation, prayer, fasting and inspirational messages from the pastors, particularly the founder Pastor Chris Oyakhilome, act as their sources of strength.

Women in Business: A Historical Overview

The involvement of women in business can be traced from time immemorial. Though their contributions have not been recognized, women have always been into trading and selling. The division of labour in the pre-colonial era, was one in which women had muscle in the economic sector. Women were active members in barter trade, selling their grains and animal skins as well clay pots in exchange for beads and other foreign products. Geiger and others illustrate that the study of pre-colonial trade and politics mention women trading with Portuguese in markets in the 16th century (Geiger *et al* 2002:172). In the same vein, Njoh gives an example of women in Yorubaland, currently Western Nigeria. For Njoh (2006:95) women were actively involved in trading and commercial activities. Hence one can note that African women were not as powerless as depicted in most biased literature written to achieve certain agendas. It has to be understood that the restriction of women in business activities was a result of the colonial policies and system of government. The colonial era succeeded in significantly altering the economic system of Africa. The Victorian image (the perception of a perfect woman by Europeans) relegated women to the private sphere, and the public was restricted to men, hence businesses and economy became male spaces.

The restriction of women in the business sector in Zimbabwe continued even after colonialism, given that the new government (the Zimbabwean Government) inherited the old system of government (from the Colonial Government). Women thus were the main victims of economic exclusion, and were confined to working in the home. This has led to the economic dependence of women on men as breadwinners, given that mostly men have had access to the means of production. Cheater notes that women have been denied access to the means of production. However, organizations such as the Indigenous Business Women Organization (IBWO) have been formed by women after realizing that they have been marginalized within existing business activities (Cheater 2003). Though they are facing challenges, women are now visible in the business space. Having discussed the general history of women in business from the precolonial era to present, I move on to discuss the involvement of Christian women in business.

Christian Women in Business

Christian women from various churches, such as African Initiated Churches, Mainline Churches or Pentecostal Churches, are actively involved in businesses. Women from the above mentioned churches are into vegetable-selling, flea markets, cross-border trading, buying and selling of foreign currency and network marketing among other businesses. Though women from other churches now engage in business activities, women from African Initiated Churches are the most commonly known Christian entrepreneurs. African Initiated Churches encourage their members to engage in business activities. Sibanda quoted by Mapuranga (2014:234) expounded that " each family (among the African Initiated Churches) is renowned for a wide range of one or more technical skills like carpentry, basketry, metal working, building and leather working. Women and children are mostly involved in the trade of homemade artefacts of their respective families."Women entrepreneurs of JohaneMarange Church are commonly known as *madzimaiemapotoerata*which literally means women (sellers) of metal pots. Mabhunu (2010) notes that economic empowerment for women is encouraged by senior female adherents who inspire them to work.

Entrepreneurship among Christian women has extended to Pentecostal churches. Buying and selling is now the order of the day among Pentecostal women from various churches. In churches such as the Zimbabwe Assemblies of God Africa (ZAOGA), almost every woman moves around with a small basket with items ranging in cost from as little as 10c; employed or unemployed women are encouraged to work with their own hands by their pastors, elders and deacons. Despite having some major business involvement, for example with flea market stalls, cross border trading and salons, women are encouraged to sell small items such as sweets, chocolates, roasted nuts etc. The rationale behind selling such small products (basket business) is that a woman must always have something in her wallet (ZAOGA F.I.F KadomaRimuka District: Ladies teachings).

Women of faith: Christ Embassy women in business

Christ Embassy women are not an exception in business issues. The gospel that is preached at Christ Embassy encourages women to work, and hence a number of them are business personnel. Some women in Christ Embassy are into a number of trades, small scale as well as large scale businesses. Other Christ Embassy women own restaurants. Yet others sell cosmetics and others are cross border traders. Some own flea market stalls and others are part of the cleaning detergents industry, among other businesses. Network marketing is yet another business that women in Christ Embassy are involved in. Though the results of interviews indicated that most women in Christ Embassy who are business women are largely unemployed women, who were not privileged enough to attain better education, in some cases, working women engage inbusiness side-by-side formal employment. Most of these women (employed) indicate that one cannot fully sustain one's self and the needs of one's family depending onsalary alone. Business works to supplement one's income.

Case 1

Mrs Nketa (not her real name) pointed that she is into restaurant business. Mrs Nketa notes that the word that they are taught in Christ Embassy encourages one to work for a giving and a living.

> The word preached by our pastor Ma (meaning Pastor Mother Ruth Musarurwa) is motivational for women to be ideal women who can sustain themselves. When l started my business, l had nothing but the word from the man of God, Pastor Chris, gave me strength. l enjoy reading Pastor Chris literature and listening to his sermons. The message in *How To Make Your Faith Work* by Pastor Christ Oyakhilome, Chapter 4 Receiving is by Faith, made me who l am today. The message helped my faith to grow and believe that l can do anything through Christ, and l can receive what l need if l put my faith to work, be it health, happy marriage as well as my business. I had nothing but faith gave me hope to start the business. With fasting and praying with my fellow sisters in Christ, God granted the desires of my heart to become a business woman. (Interview, Mrs Nketa, 05–06-15).

Mrs Nketa owns three restaurants in Harare, one in Kuwadzana Extension, the other two in town (Harare CBD). She indicated that as a single and unemployed woman, it is money from her businesses that she is using to take care of her family and she indicated that her two daughters are at a boarding school. (Interview Mrs Nketa 05-06-15).

Not only married women in Christ Embassy are into business. Girls are also trained to become better and responsible future mothers. A number of Christ Embassy girls in Harare are business women. Some of them are college students, yet they run some business, though relatively small scale businesses. Some sell cosmetics, jewellery and clothing, and others are involved with network marketing groups like Green World, Amway and Tiens which sell a number of products ranging from tablets to health teas and cosmetics. Others sell Avon beauty products. (Group Interview Greendale Assembly 07-06-15).

Case 2

Sister Tariro, an unmarried 23 year-old woman, is in the cosmetic business. She sells lipstick, jewellery and perfumes, as well as ladies' beauty lotions and creams.

> Though l have challenges of time in my business because I'm a student, this trade has been a source of blessing, and it has helped me survive college life as a decent woman. I never aspired to have a sugar daddy, so as to get money for shopping, my hair and nails, because I have never lacked. My business sustains me to do my shopping as a woman, as well as my groceries at school. How I started my business: I can testify it as God's grace. I realized my position as a Child of God that l must not lack. From Pastor Chris' sermons on LoveWorld T.V station, I understood the power of anointing. I realized that anointing is the ability to do what you cannot do. Though I knew it could be difficult to run a business, I stood by the power of anointing. I suspended reasoning and ignored the stress of where I could get the resources to buy my products. Anointing gave me faith to hope for what l could not see, such faith gave me confidence and boldness to start my business (Interview Sister Tariro 01-06-15).

Case 3

Mai Nyuke, a senior member of Christ Embassy church, is involved with the network marketing business. She is a member of Tiens, a Chinese Network company which sells health products such as tablets and teas. She indicated that:

A fellow sister in Christ who is a member of Tiens convinced me to join the business. At first I was hesitant to join with an understanding of the criticism that people direct towards such Chinese products.

The products are criticised as *zvitiyi nezvimapiritsizvemaChaina*(Chinese teas and herbs) which literally means inefficient Chinese herb tea and tablets.

> I doubted the business given the general perception of the herbs by the majority. Initially, around the same time I was approached by this sister, we were in a week of prayer and fasting, I could continuously hear a voice saying 'I can do all things through Christ who strengthens me', and sometimes I could ignore the voice,till I realized that it was the voice of the Lord that was giving me strength. I joined the network and kept reading scriptures. Luke 1:37, which states that nothing is impossible with God as long as you believe and 1 Corinthians 15:58, which states that one must remain steadfast and unmoveable because God rewards one's labour, became my inspirational verses and point of strength.The Pastor's message for that whole week seemed to be directed at me. This gave me so much faith. I meditated upon Hebrews 11, understanding how the wishes of great people in the Bible were granted only by faith. I began hoping for the substance I could not see (Hebrew 11:1). Faith created a picture of a big network market, I started selling the products and having other members joining under me. My network has grown and I am now a 6 star business owner. I now get a salary from Tiens which is calculated from my network monthly sales. (Interview 24–05-15).

Although only three cases have been presented for an in-depth appreciation of the dynamics, many women are into various kinds of businesses in Christ Embassy. Some are vendors in Chinhoyi Street in Harare. They sell vegetables, compact discs and groceries. Others sell second-hand clothes commonly known as *mabhero*. Cross-border trading is yet another trade women in Christ Embassy are into. They import clothes, handbags and shoes from South Africa, Botswana, Tanzania, China and Dubai. One woman reports that she is in the cleaning detergent industry, she makes dishwashing liquid as well as toilet cleaning chemicals. (Group Interview 24–05-15).

An analysis of the above interviewed women indicates that women at Christ Embassy Church in Harare in particular are into different kinds of businesses. Some businesses are large scale others are small scale. Women of different age groups and from different social classes engage in business activities. Class, however, is the major factor that causes the differences in businesses women engage in. Women from the upper class, particularly those from low density suburbs such as Greendale, Borrowdale, Belvedere, Avondale and Chisipite among other areas, are into large-scale businesses, given their social setting and ability to afford running such businesses. Women from the lower classes engage in small-scale businesses. Research indicated that women from Mbare, Mufakose, Chitungwiza and Kuwadzana normally engage in businesses like vending, selling vegetables, airtime, and second hand clothes *mabhero*among other types of businesses. One, therefore, can conclude that the kind of business one engages in (in most cases) is determined by one's class or social status.

Despite being from different classes, these women are all influenced by the same factor to engage in business. Whether poor or rich, young or old, faith is the major drive that powers them. Faith is their key source of hope, confidence, motivation and inspiration to engage in various businesses.Their basis of faith is in the Bible and Pastor Chris' sermons and books. Messages in the *Rhapsody of Realities,* which circulates every month with a message for each day, is yet another point of reference for women in Christ Embassy to find strength to engage in business. Sermons, prayers and confessions in the *Rhapsody of Realities*are motivational for church members, and women sometimes interpret the messages to suit their situation. For instance, the message can be interpreted in a way that suits their business activities. Mrs Nketa notes that the confession in the *Rhapsody of Realities* May 2015 for Wednesday the 6th motivated and gave her confidence. "All things are mine! I walk in the reality of my inheritance in Christ today! My life is upward and forward only! I'm not moved by inflation, economic downturns and meltdowns, because l play by a different set of rules! I'm an heir of God with complete access to an incorruptible inheritance!" (Oyakhilome May 2015). Mrs Nketa stressed that, looking at the economic situation in Zimbabwe, she was at a point of quitting her business, but after she meditated upon the above confession in the *Rhapsody of Realities,* her strength was renewed and faith powered her to keep going in business (Interview Mrs Nketa 05-06-15).

Spirituality, thus, is always a source of hope and confidence for women to stand. Such power based on spirituality can be traced to the 11th century (the proto-feminist era) in Christianity. Women were not allowed to preach because of the patriarchal nature of their societies, but certain women claimed mysticism as their source of power. Women such as Hildegard of Bingen, Mary Astell, Margret Fell and Julian of Norwich claimed their power to speak through mysticism (Wood 2012). In the same vein, despite the discouragement that women get from some men when they want to engage in businesses activities, faith continues to be their source of power and inspiration.

Sources of Hope for Women in Christ Embassy

The Bible, prayer, fasting, confessions, pastor's sermons (in most cases Pastor Chris'), as well as books are sources of hope for Christ Embassy members to boost their faith. Songs are also relevant as they carry a message of anticipation. Many Christians generally believe that faith changes a situation. Adelegan (2013:255) expounded that "faith activates the anointing and ignites the power of God. Once the anointing takes over, it's beyond reasoning. It drives fear and doubt away and makes available more than enough power to help you achieve the things you plan to achieve." The above mentioned sources of hope are elements that boost one's faith. Women in Christ Embassy have been and continue to be motivated through meditating upon the Bible and Pastor Chris' literature. In addition, prayer and fasting, as well as songs encourage them to press on. These give them confidence and boost their morale so that they to take part in business activities. Below I examine these sources of inspiration for Christ Embassy women in business in some detail.

The Bible

In almost all religions the status and authority of sacred scriptures is unquestionable. Sacred scriptures may be regarded as manuals which contain solutions to all matters that pertain to human life. In Islam the Koran is treated with reverence, while in Christianity the Bible is the most consecrated book and it is sacrosanct. The Bible is understood to be the word of God. 1 Timothy 3:16 clearly states that scriptures are inspired. The text is perceived by certain Christians to contain answers to all issues, including health, sickness or war, as well as economic ones. Vengeyi (2013) outlines that the Bible, for the Christians, is not just a heap of pages, but it has powers in itself. It is more like a manual and it has ready-made answers to human problems. Women thus use the Bible to reclaim their economic space. They get motivation from the biblical texts.

Certain scriptures which relate to women in business are cited by many women. Proverbs 31:10-13 continues to be a widely quoted reference which depicts an ideal woman who is obedient and hardworking.

> Who can find a virtuous wife?...She seeks wool and flax and she willingly works with her hands... she also rises while it is yet night and provides food for her household. She perceives that her merchandise is good...she makes linen garments and sells them, and supplies sashes for the merchants... she does not eat the bread of idleness (Proverbs 31:10-31).

This verse has empowered women to engage in business activities. Women at Christ Embassy Church Harare, despite their social differences, desire to be the kind of a woman who works for her family. For Smith (2008) an idealized view of women's economic activities appears in Proverbs 31. Mrs Mujinga, (not her real name) of Christ Embassy Mbare Cell group, in line with Proverbs 31:10-31, indicated that:

> *Mudzimai akakwana anoonekwa nekushandira mhuri yake mukubudikidza nekuita mabhindauko akasiyanasiyana. Varume vanhasi havadi vakadzi vakaneta muviri vanokumbira kese-kese. Ini pachangu chichi nekunzvera shoko zvakandibatsira kuti ndive mukadzi anoziva kuzvishandira nemaoko ake.*

This translates to:

> An ideal woman is seen to work for her family, getting out and doing different tasks. Men of today do not want idle women, who always are begging. In my own case, the Church and meditating upon the word helped me to become a woman who knows how to work with her own hands. (Interview Mai Mujinga 11-06-15).

From the above, one can be convinced that religion has a role to play in women's engagement in business. Their faith thus has motivated them to be women who work with their hands. An ideal woman in Proverbs 31:10-31 acts as the role model that women ought to follow. Despite the ups and downs they face in trying to achieve the goal of becoming businesswomen, women endure in faith. As mentioned earlier, there are a number of verses that are cited by women to drive them into business. Though some verses do not directly address business, they are interpreted in a manner that suits the context.

Prayer and Fasting

Prayer is believed to be the panacea for all problems by many Christians. Being powered by faith to engage in business issues, women in Christ Embassy have realized that their answers are in praying as well as fasting. Women in Christ Embassy fast and pray for the growth of their already established businesses, as well as for those who are about to start. "I have a prayer partner whom l usually fast and pray with every Monday and Wednesday for the divine intervention of God in our businesses." (Interview 07–06-15). Praying and fasting thus play avital role in the participation of Christ Embassy women in businesses. Women gain boldness and confidence in praying and fasting. Pastors also pray for businesses to flourish. In one of the services the researcher attended, Christ Embassy Zimbabwe zonal Pastor, Ruth Musarurwa, prayed for members with business issues. She prayed for successes in business. (Sunday Service 24–05-15, Christ Embassy Belvedere).

Sermons

Sermons have a role to play in driving women to participate in business. Their strong belief in the words from their pastors drives them. Though Christ Embassy members listen to sermons from other pastors, it is the sermons from Pastor Chris that largely motivate them. Sermons by Pastor Chris on Love World Television give assurance to members that what is deemed impossible can be possible through faith. Miracles and testimonies on TV also create the zeal of "doing things by God's grace." Pastor Chris stresses the faith gospel. Gifford (2004) illustrates that Chris is one pastor who emphasizes the faith gospel, and encourages his members not to be influenced by what surrounds them. For Pastor Chris, as noted by Gifford (2004), one must simply ignore his or her situation and simply believe what the Bible says. This, hence, has driven a number of women to engage in business despite their economic hardships. Pastor Chris in one of his sermons says, "Stop wondering what is happening to my business. Nothing bad is happening to your business. The one who brought you this far is extremely faithful." In the same vein he adds that "God is the Chairman of my business" (Gifford 2004:145). Having the assurance from "the man of God," women's faith in the words of the man of God drive them into buying and selling.

Ruth Musarurwa (zonal Pastor) preached a sermon which was motivational to business people. "Anointing has the power to beautify your business. In every business there is going to be a quick start, *kana uchitengesamadomasiuchatengesa witha difference* (if you are selling tomatoes you are going to sell them with a difference)" (Ruth Musarurwa, sermon 24-06-15 12.25pm). Such sermons energize women to participate in trading and selling with confidence in God's word. One woman interviewed notes that she also gained confidence in some of the songs that are sung in Christ Embassy. "I love the song called *you are a Miracle God*. Its lyrics give hope. The song gives the confidence that God is a miracle God and it all belongs to him, and knowing for sure that God is my father and I'm an heir therefore l will never lack what l desire because my father (God) owns the world." (Interview 11-06-15).

Pastor Chris Oyakhilome's Literature

Though the Bible is the widely treasured book whose words are valued by most Christians, the reverence given to Pastor Chris' literature by Christ Embassy members should not be overlooked. As the founder of the church, whatever he utters is appreciated. Members of the church are of the contention that Pastor Chris is a true man of God, hence some believe that whatever he teaches are inspired words from God. Christ Embassy believers refer to pastor Chris' literature for spiritual edification, comfort, hope and strength. Women in business make use of such literature to gain confidence and boost their source of power to engage in business, which is faith. Pastor Chris has a number of books that have driven women to engage into business as well as becoming strong and confident business-women. A book entitled *Wisdom for Women* contains a message of encouragement for women. In this book Pastor Chris notes that women must learn to do things right, if they want to be successful in business. He adds that it is the word and the life of God that make circumstances bow to one's dictates (Oyakhilome 1998:37). One may, therefore, be convinced that words from the man of God which are faith-based energize women to engage in business activities. Apart from *Wisdom for Women*, Pastor Chris authored *How to Pray Effectively* and *How To Make Your Faith Work* among others. These books were reported by some interviewed women in Christ Embassy Belvedere to be manuals for a perfect life.

> These books, I tell you, are a guide to a smooth life. *Wisdom for Women* was one of the presents that I got from my mother at my kitchen party before my wedding, and it continues to inspire me as a young woman. *How To Pray Effectively* has taught me the right way of praying, now, I believe that the key to every problem is prayer. Having learned on how to make faith work after reading a book by our pastor, *How To Make Your Faith Work,* I practised it and, my sister, I testify that it worked. I had to start my business with nothing, I felt pregnant for my business (putting faith to work) knowing that I will give birth to it. I suspended reasoning, faith was the only factor that was driving me. My miracle took place. My sister who is in Australia, sent me US $2000 to start something, l had never asked for that money. The only thing I did was to put my faith to work. This might sound funny but it's true. I had already planned my business on paper, and waited for the capital, which I had no idea as to where it was going to come from (Interview Anonymous 12–06-15).

From the above interview, one can appreciate the motivational nature of Pastor Chris' literature for Christ Embassy members. A discussion of Pastor Chris' literature could not be complete without referring to his most popular and most read literature, the *Rhapsody of Realities*. *Rhapsody of Realities* is a daily devotional which circulates every month, with sermons, prayers, confessions and a Bible reading plan for each day, from the first to the last day of the month. This literature is also inspiring for women, challenging them to gain boldness in business. One interviewed woman highlighted that the *Rhapsody of Realities* sermon dated Thursday 21 May 2015 was a sermon of words defining one's life 'Your Words Define Your Life'. Chengeto (not her real name) notes that though the sermon was not directed at business issues, for her it had implications for motivating her in her commitment to business.

> I got motivated with the confessions attached to the sermon. I liked the part that indicated that "my words are wholesome, and they are producing life to my body, job, business, ministry, family, and all that concerns me." It gave me confidence that even businesses are God-governed and l should not worry because God is always in control (Interview Chengeto 07–06-15).

This section presented evidence that the Bible, praying and fasting, pastors' sermons and literature ignited faith in Christ Embassy women and such faith is what drove them to engage in business activities. A number of women in Christ Embassy are into business through the motivation of faith. Having discussed the above, the next section is going to focus on the challenges faced by women in business.

Challenges Faced by Christ Embassy Women in Business

Women generally face a number of challenges in the business field. The cultural understanding of economic space as a male space is one of the greatest challenges women face. Thus, women who crossover to the presumed male domain are stereotyped as women of loose morals. One can, therefore, agree with Mauchi *et al* (2014) that culture affects the success of women entrepreneurs. Because of patriarchal thinking that men must always dominate and be breadwinners, some men feel threatened if women engage in business and generate money. Chopamba (2010:22) thus, notes that barriers that undermine the economic and social emancipation of women are in line with their traditional culture. One woman from Christ Embassy indicated that, her husband did not permit her to go out of the country, thus her cross border trading business was about to be in jeopardy until she got a revelation from God to work with her sister, who now goes out of the country and brings back the goods for selling (Interview 07-06-15). Though the involvement of women in various forms of economic entrepreneurship enhances their social and financial freedom (Gabay and Death 2014:56), some men tend to demoralize their wives because of jealousy and are eager to dominate.

Capital is yet another problem women encounter in business. Most women face financial constraints. Data collected in this study has indicated the majority of women entrepreneurs used to depend on their husband's income, hence capital to start the businesses was a problem, given that some men were against the involvement of their wives in business activities. Apart from failing to get funding from their husbands, women sometimes cannot access credits or loans from formal institutions because of their limited access to formal education, ownership of property and social mobility (Mauchi *et al* 2014:468). Loan and credit institutions do not usually give money to women, as most of them lack collateral. However, there are some institutions that offer loans to groups or women cooperatives, but the challenge still remains, given that not every woman can access such funds.

Married women encounter the problem of a double burden when they are into business activities. Household responsibilities of caring for the children, as well as household chores, place demands on women (Mathapo 2001). Because of the dual burden, many women, therefore, fail to give adequate time to their business, unlike their male counterparts. Though some resort to looking for housemaids, for others it remains a challenge, as their husbands do not permit employing house-helps. Some women interviewed reported that they could not employ housemaids as their husbands do not allow their clothes to be washed and ironed, nor their food to be prepared by someone else (Group Interview 24-05-15). Such burdens lead to the challenge of lack of networking. Mauchi *et al* indicate that networking is yet another challenge faced by businesswomen. Women are not able to travel far and wide and engage in networking due to the responsibilities that they have (Mauchi *et al* 2014:476).

Women businesses in general are affected by lack of confidence and the fear of risk taking. Mauchi *et al* (2014:471) note that "due to lack of technical skills, confidence, strong individual involvement and willingness to take risks, women are often unable to establish and sustain successful businesses. Risk taking is indicated as a key characteristic for successful entrepreneurship, yet women are not risk takers" (Mauchi *et al* 2014:471). Though these are indicated as challenges faced by women in business, it has to be appreciated that Christ Embassy women are enduring in faith. Without capital, as indicated earlier on, women in Christ Embassy make business plans with the faith that their God will provide for them. Faith empowers women to take risks and engage in business.

In spite of the general perception that women lack confidence in businesses, faith has been and continues to be a source of power which gives them strength, confidence and boldness to engage in trade. Despite the challenges that they encounter, women are motivated by faith, a factor that drives them to be businesswomen. Christ Embassy women engage in businesses for various reasons. For some the goal is to become economically independent from men, thus exercising their financial freedom. For others, the motive is to supplement their husbands' income. Some working class women indicated that their motive was complementing their salaries with business profits, among other factors. Though these women differ in motives, they are all are empowered by faith. Although religious attitudes are sometimes factors that hinder women's involvement in business, it has to be understood that Christ Embassy doctrines promote and support female entrepreneurship, as indicated by the above interviews.

Conclusion

Women are driven by a number factors to engage in business activities. The desire to be economically independent has pushed women to be involved with capital-generating entities. Upon realizing that their economic dependence on men is one of the causes of some of the domestic abuses by men, women are striving to be businesswomen. The Zimbabwean economy as well, has a role to play in the involvement of women in business. With the economic crisis and hardship in Zimbabwe most men carry a burden as breadwinners. Thus, women are complimenting their husbands' salaries with their businesses. A major force for Pentecostal women in business in Zimbabwe has been faith. Pentecostal women are being faith-driven to engage in business activities. Faith has been and continues to be their motivator and source of hope, strength and confidence, as shown in the case of Christ Embassy women in Harare.

Being powered by faith to be business women, Christ Embassy women have become and are becoming prominent sales people in Harare. The Bible, sermons and Pastor Chris' literature as well as praying and fasting, give them confidence in business. Despite the challenges that they encounter in the economic sector as business women, ranging from the cultural definition of the public space as male space, the need for capital to start a business, the double burden of business and the pressures of motherhood among other factors, women endure with faith as their ground of confidence, hope and strength. Given this, the role of religious doctrines in the economic empowerment of women should not be overlooked. Religion is therefore performing a major role in promoting women entrepreneurs.

References

Adelegan, F. (2013), *Nigeria's Leading Lights of the Gospel Revolutionaries in Worldwide Christianity*, Bloomington: West Bow Press.

Allaman, J., Geiger, S. and Musisi, N. (2002), *Women in African Colonial Histories*, Bloomington: Indiana University Press.

Cheater, A. (2003), *The Anthropology of Power*, New York: Routledge.

Chopamba, L. (2010), *The Struggle for Economic Support of the Indiginous (sic) Business Women in Zimbabwe*, Bloomington: Xilbris Corporation.

Gabay, C. & Death, C. (2014), *Critical Perspectives on African Politics, Liberal Inventions, State building and Civil society*, New York: Routledge.

Gifford, P. (2004), *Ghana's New Christianity: Pentecostalism in a globalizing African Economy*, London: C Hurst & Co Publishers.

Gopal, G. &Salim, M. (1998), *Gender and Law: Eastern Africa Speaks: Proceedings of The Conference Organized by the World Bank & Economic Commission for Africa*, Washington: W B Publications.

Mapuranga, T.P. (2014), 'Surviving the Urban Jungle: African Initiated Churches and Women's Socio-Economic Coping Strategies in Harare 2000-2010', in E. Chitando, J. Kugler and M.R Gunda (eds.), *Multiplying In The Spirit: African Initiated Churches In Zimbabwe*, Bamberg: Bamberg University Press.

Mathapo, T.G. (2001), 'Profiling and Identifying Challenges facing women in small business in Capricon District Municipality', Project submitted in partial fulfilment of the requirements for the Degree of Master in Business Adminstration, *Unpublished thesis*: Limpopo University.

Mauchi, F.N, Mutengezanwa, M. and Damiyano, D. (2014), 'Challenges Faced by Women Entrepreneurs: A Case Study of Mashonaland Central Province, *International Journal of Development and Sustainability*, Vol 3.3, 466–480.

Njoh, A.J. (2006), *Tradition, Culture and Development in Africa: Historical Lessons for Modern Development Planning*, Surrey: Ashgate Pubishing Ltd.

Oyakhilome, A. (1998), *Wisdom for Women*, Lagos: Love World Publication.

Oyakhilome, C. (2007), *How To Make Your Faith Work*, Lagos: Love World Publishing Ministry.

Oyakhilome, C. (2015), *Rhapsody of Realities. . . A Daily Devotional*, Lagos: Love World Publishing.

Smith, B.N. (2008), *The Oxford Encyclopaedia of Women in World History*, Vol 4, Oxford University Press.

Vengeyi O. (2011), 'Gona and the Bible among Indigenous Pentecostal Churches of Zimbabwe: A Comparative Approach', in Gunda, M.R (ed), *From Text to Practice The Role of The Bible in the Daily Living of African People Today*, BiAS 4, Bamberg, University of Bamberg Press.

Wood, J. M. (2012), 'Patriarchy, feminism and Mary Daly: A systematic theological enquiry into Daly's engagement with gender issues in Christian Theology', Unpublished PhD Thesis, Pretoria: UNISA.

Interviews (all the names used are pseudonyms)

Sister Tariro, a young lady who goes to Christ Embassy Church, 01 June 2015, Ebony Hair Salon, Harare

Mai Mujinga, Christ Embassy member, 11 June 2015, CBD Harare

Mai Nyuke, Christ Embassy member, 24 May 2015, CBD Harare

Group Interview 24 May 2015, Christ Embassy Belvedere, Harare

Mrs Nketa, member of Christ Embassy, 05 June 2015, KuwadzanaExtention, Harare

Group Interview, 07 June 2015, Greendale, Harare

Chengeto, Christ Embassy member, 07 June 2015, Marlborough, Harare

Anonymous, Christ Embassy member, 09 June 2015, CBD, Harare

Easter Kawara, Christ Embassy member, 11 June 2015, Telephone Interview

Sister Agnella, Christ Embassy member, 12 June 2015, Telephone Interview

Sermons

Ladies Teaching ZAOGA FIF, 2013, Rimuka District, Kadoma

Pastor Ruth Musarurwa, Preaching, 24 May 2015- 12.25pm, Christ Embassy Belvedere, Harare

Sunday Service, 24 May 2015 Christ Embassy Belvedere, Harare.

CHAPTER 7

Mbiri Kuna Jesu: Pentecostal Women's Economic Participation In Harare

The Case Of Prophetic, Healing And Deliverance Ministries

TABONA SHOKO

Introduction

THIS CHAPTER DISCUSSES WOMEN's economic participation in the Prophetic, Healing and Deliverance Ministries (PHD) in Harare. Founded in 2013 by Prophet Walter Magaya in Harare, the church emerged at a time of Zimbabwe's economic challenges. This followed a period of hyper inflation that stemmed from Zimbabwe's policies of land reform in 2000. The policy led to economic decline and caused hyper inflation that led to shortages of basic commodities such as electricity, fuel, food stuffs and cash in the banks. This situation was compounded by economic sanctions against the country imposed by Western countries and this led to misery, depression and despair amongst most people. As a result, Zimbabwean Christians were not spared, and many churches have been formed for spiritual nourishment and solace. Under this climate, the PHD was formed. As is typical of Pentecostal movements, the church preached the gospel of prosperity and adherents embarked on entrepreneurship. As a result, women and young professionals, who form the bulk of the members of the church, have been involved in economic ventures through cross border trading, running flea markets, foreign exchange activities, sales of bales of clothes, shoes, etc in Harare. This chapter, therefore, explores the role that the Pentecostal church plays in the lives of women's economic lives of women in Harare. It argues that many women develop an interesting relationship between work and religion as they feel that the social networks and self confidence they gain from their religious communities are as important as their spiritual experiences. However, not all the women who join the church remain as members. Based on empirical research, the chapter explores why some women leave the church in which they had previously felt that they gained so much.

There has been a growing interest on Pentecostal studies in Africa. In Zimbabwe, the studies have focused on Pentecostal church healing. Shoko (2009) captures the thrust of scholarship on Pentecostal churches in Zimbabwe. Some prominent scholars include Paul Gifford (1988) who explored the political and economic role played by Pentecostal churches in politics in Southern Africa. Gifford attributes the phenomenon of Pentecostalism to social and psychological alienation of certain aspects of modernity. David Maxwell's (2005) case study of the Zimbabwe Assemblies of God Africa (ZAOGA), sets out to demonstrate how Pentecostalism exerts a quest for satisfaction for social malcontents in neo-liberal Zimbabwe. Although Maxwell studied the nature of Pentecostal spirituality, as well as examining the relationship between Pentecostalism and politics in ZAOGA, he did not pay particular attention to Pentecostal healing (Shoko 2009: 42). Kudzai Biri (2012) also explored the phenomenon of healing in ZAOGA. Clearly, the issue of women and their participation in the economy has not received much attention. This chapter seeks to explore the women's role in the economy in Harare. The chapter starts by explaining the phenomenon of prophecy in Zimbabwe, proceeds to deal with PHD and Gospel of Prosperity and the women's involvement in economic activities in Harare.

Prophecy in Zimbabwe

There has been an avalanche of prophecy generated by Pentecostal Churches in Zimbabwe. These are churches that preach the gospel of prosperity, healing and deliverance through the performance of miracles. Some prominent Pentecostal Churches that have germinated in Zimbabwe recently include Prophet Emmanuel Makandiwa's UFIC, Uebert Angel's Spirit Embassy and Prophet Walter Magaya's PHD Ministries. Makandiwa and Angel claim to receive anointing from their spiritual father, the Ghanaian Prophet Victor Kusi Boateng. Also popular in Zimbabwe is Prophet TB Joshua of Nigeria. Magaya has claimed the Synagogue Church of All Nations (Scoan) leader Temitope Balogun (TB) Joshua is his "spiritual father," and at one time invited the Nigerian cleric to Zimbabwe, a claim he (TB Joshua) vehemently dismissed as 'dream' (News Day Zimbabwe 10/04/14). This mad rush for prophecy in Zimbabwe has also attracted some high profile Cabinet ministers, who have visited local and foreign prophets in the past few years to have their problems solved.

Young professional women too have not been spared in this mad rush. Despite much scepticism about Pentecostal churches' miraculous healings, gold falling from space, and all sorts of wonders, people have been attracted to the gospel of prosperity. Analysts observe that poverty levels in Zimbabwe tend to push citizens to go for an easier 'prophecy' route. And most people who prefer prophets are poor and that social ills were caused by failed economic policies. Magaya himself said that many people were losing their valuables to the gospel of prosperity; "This gospel of prosperity is robbing ordinary people of their hard-earned cash" (*Zim Diaspora* 29/07/13). Be that as it may, many people, particularly women and the youth, form that majority of Pentecostal church adherents. They have varied reasons for joining, but most share expectations such as being healed of illnesses, finding jobs, and other personal expectations such as finding a potential life partner. Influenced by the gospel of prosperity, many women engage in economic activities in various ways. At this point it is important to discuss the foundation of PHD Ministries and the Gospel of Prosperity before we deal with women's economic ventures.

PHD Ministries

The Prophetic, Healing and Deliverance Ministries (PHD) is a Bible-based community of believers who gather together to worship the LORD and to take back what the devil has stolen from God's people. Headquartered in Harare, Zimbabwe, PHD Ministries' main purpose is to bring Physical, Spiritual and Economic deliverance to all that are oppressed by the devil (http://www.phdministries.org, Accessed 5/05/15). The church was founded by Prophet Walter Magaya in Harare in 2014, after breaking away from the Roman Catholic Church. The Prophet Magaya claims his mentor is the famous Nigerian prophet, Prophet T.B Joshua, who acts as his spiritual father. The Pentecostal church shares many of the Pentecostal churches characteristics; that is it is 'spirit-type', meaning it places great emphasis on the outpouring of the Holy Spirit on the Day of Pentecost; members believe they are 'born again' and speak in tongues. The church specialises in prophesy, healing and delivering people from bondages and calamities both spiritual and physical. (Shoko 2009: 48). One church adherent traces its history of origins as having "started with a small membership in Chitungwiza, it then moved to the city of Harare and then finally established at Zindoga Shopping Centre in Waterfalls. Here it has established its headquarters in refurbished warehouse in the industrial site. According to Mundondo, at the time of writing it was one of the churches that had the biggest membership in Harare which exceeded 10 000 people per service. It had a very big gathering, an all-night prayer on 7 November 2014, called "A Night of Turn Around" which had over three hundred thousand people from all over the world (Mundondo 2015: 19).

Church attendance is concentrated in Harare. The members feel that that the prophet Magaya has tremendous power to perform wonders and as a result people visit from faraway places such as Beitbridge in the Southern part of the country, Kariba in the North, Mutare in the East and Bulawayo in the West. At the time of writing, Magaya's popularity had also reached some people in neighbouring SADC countries like Mozambique South Africa, Zambia and Botswana. The concentration in Harare is based on the strong belief that prophetic power is concentrated most at the place where the prophet resides, and the further one is from the prophet, the less effective the miracles. As such, PHD church has not spread to other parts of the country and its headquarters remains its main church in Waterfalls. But, in some small way the church has managed to spread to other parts of the country through its membership in cell groups. The groups comprise small groups of believers who gather in houses in the evenings during week days, particularly Wednesdays, to pray. The members pay subscriptions and membership fees and they appoint their lordship structures such as Chairperson, Secretary and Treasurer. Some members are so influential such that they exert power which mimics that of prophet Magaya. The cell groups are reached out to by the prophet through crusades and sometimes members come to attend the night prayers.

Hierarchy

The organisation of the PHD ministries is highly stratified. At the top of the hierarchy is Magaya who is the Prophet and serves as the instrument of God. The prophet wields tremendous power; he is endowed with the gift of prophesy, speaking in tongues, delivering people from all calamities and healing (Mundondo 2015: 20). Although PHD ministries is a church that was co-founded with Magaya and his wife, Tendai, the Prophet's wife is not called a Prophetess or other honorific titles such as those used for prophets' wives in other Pentecostal churches. Rather Tendai is called 'mother'. She does not preach, heal or prophesy. In fact, she is almost invisible in the church activities. She is visible during charity work when the ministry will be donating to the old aged, orphans and under privileged people of the society. Following the footprints of Tendai, there are very few women in PHD who hold influential positions in the church. But close scrutiny shows that Magaya's wife, despite her invisibility, carries the title, 'amai' which translates to 'mother.' This term wields immense covert power in Shona traditional society. The implication is that Tendai, despite her not featuring in the public sphere, remains very powerful behind the scenes.

Apart from the prophet perched at the top of the hierarchy, there are some junior pastors who help out the prophet during the ministries. These are men whose main task is to deliver and to anoint people, but they do not hold power to prophesy. Besides serving as pastors, men in PHD ministry have influential positions such as cell group leaders, finance personnel, security guards, ushers, prophet's body guards, information and technology personnel (Mundondo 2015: 20). One example of an influential men is Oscar Pambuka who is a prominent journalist and is the spokesperson of the church. Women's roles are minor and include house decoration, ushering, translating, medical team, singing in the present worship and in rare cases counselling (Mundondo 2015: 20).

Beliefs

Prophet Magaya is a unique Prophet in the sense that although he is an instrument of God, initially he did not make reference to or cite quotations from the Bible. His belief is that he simply serves as God's messenger, and does not manufacture things of his own making (Maposa interview 10/04/15). However in PHD ministries, there are many beliefs which the 'man of God' Magaya and the membership strongly uphold, such as the power of the anointing oil. The oil is so precious to the ministry that it is perceived as 'holy oil' and is called the 'Resurrection Anointing Oil'. One adherent claimed that it is based on the Bible (James 5:14) which says that it was supposed to be given to sick people. But unlike the biblical oil that is only confined to use by the sick, theirs is open to other uses such as business, social and political in order to break the chains of the devil. Because of its perceived efficacy, members call it, "The Father of All" (Pambuka interview 25/03/15).

PHD ministries members also believe in the anointed artefacts such as wrist bands, T-shirts, caps, umbrellas and badges. They believe that these items can protect a believer against spiritual and physical harm caused by *varoyi* (witches). They also design stickers and calendars that are used to protect homes, cars, furniture and laptops against infiltration by the devil. Members also believe in anointed books that are also read in order to increase wisdom, while the guest house and holy ground deliver people from spiritual attacks (Mandizha interview 25.03/15). In fact members believe that illness and disease in this world can be pin-pointed to Satan, the arch-enemy of God, malignant spirits and witchcraft. Many members attribute serious illnesses and diseases to the activities of witches, wizards and sorcerers. As an interviewee pointed out,

> "witches have a variety of ways at their disposal in their nefarious practice ... They have mysterious powers through which they coerce nature spirits to aid them. Thus, they manipulate *zvidhoma*, *zvitupwani*, (capricious witches' familiars), *nyoka* (snakes), *mapere* (hyenas), *hurekure* (birds) and *mazizi* (owls) and use them to harm people" (Shambare P. interview 30/03/15).

Belief in witchcraft is so real to members of the church that most of them also sprinkle water around their homesteads, and wash daily using holy oil in order to neutralise the power and potency of witchcraft. It is this aspect of belief that led some members of the Apostolic grouping to accuse Magaya of being demonic and to argue that he gets his power to treat people from snakes *(News Day* 9/02/15).

Gospel of Prosperity

PHD, like many Pentecostal churches, emphasises material prosperity by impressing upon the believers the need to live healthy fulfilled lives. They teach people using biblical texts that they will enjoy peace and prosperity if they remain faithful to God. They also claim that the true Christian has to ask for these things so that they will be granted. By contrast, if the believer does not get them, it is either because they have not asked for them or that sin has prevented them from getting the blessings (Shoko 2009: 43). Bradley A. Koch [2009:1] also defines the Prosperity Gospel as the doctrine that God wants people to be prosperous, especially financially. Adherents of this Gospel believe that wealth is a sign of God's blessing and the poor are poor because they lack faith. They interpret the New Testament as portraying Jesus as a relatively rich figure who used his wealth to feed the masses on several occasions and to finance what they argue to be a fairly expensive ministry (Mundondo 2015: 10). According to R. Akoko, this Gospel of prosperity is an American creation. Its historical development is traceable through well-known evangelists like E.W. Kenyon, A.A. Allen, Oral Roberts, T.L. Osborn, Kenneth Hagin, Kenneth Copeland, etc. The Pentecostals encourage the 'believers' to work hard and accumulate wealth that could be used to prosper the Church (Akoko 2002: 370). Magaya's PHD ministries has embraced this gospel and it is used in spreading the prosperity theology through literature, pamphlets, crusades, night vigils, CDs and any other convenient means. However, Allan Anderson has noted that many large Pentecostal and Charismatic churches appeal primarily to 'younger, educated urban people' (Anderson 2004: 159). Some of them have been sharply criticised for propagating a 'prosperity gospel' that seems to reproduce North American capitalism in disguise.

Some features of Gospel of prosperity include spirituality, healing, prophecy testimonies, offering, speaking in tongues, prayers and faith which results in material prosperity and good health (Gbote and Kgatla 2014:6–7). Faith is the quality which is most emphasized in the Gospel of Prosperity.

Tenets of Faith

Faith is of paramount importance to PHD ministries. It plays a vital role in prosperity gospel and overturning the power of Satan. The church locates the tenet of faith as cardinal to one's salvation and prosperity. According to Magaya, Satan uses his greatest weapon, which is fear, to paralyse a believer such that he/she doubts the power of God. Because of this doubt the believer cannot reap the fruits of the Gospel. Rather he/she reaps poverty. For Magaya, the disbelief is caused by lack of knowledge, tradition and natural sense. Members are misled by traditional rituals and sacrifices to evil spirits masquerading as ancestors. This is the road or beginning of getting stray in the wilderness of the devil. In the light of this false belief that obsesses humanity, he therefore calls upon people to call 'Jehovah my Banner' or 'Shield' (Exodus 17:15) so that He takes charge of one's life. Other terms that Magaya coins in his jargon include, 'Jehovah my Provider' (Genesis 22:13-14) implying that hat he miraculously provides, 'Jehovah Shammah' (Isaiah 60:19-20), meaning God is ever present in life 'Jehovah the Conqueror' who never loses any battle, 'Jehovah the Healer' and 'Jehovah Shalom' who brings Peace (Mundondo 2015: 21). These terms are popular in Zimbabwean Pentecostalism.

Thus, faith is the hall mark of a believer. Sickness is traceable to lack of faith in God. "God protects His own" (Magaya sermon 08/02/2015). According to the prophet, lack of faith in God constitutes a potential cause of misfortune, sickness and death. He is of the conviction that whoever upholds the Christian faith is unlikely to suffer from any problem. This conviction is derived from the Bible and underlies Pentecostal church belief, "Those who believe shall be saved, those who do not believe shall be condemned." (Mark 16:16). As such, his concept of salvation is the "here-and-now" and, securing membership in his church guards against problems. This is similar to ideas in some African Independent Churches (Shoko 2006:130). Magaya also demonstrates how faith works through Christ's prayer, *"Our Father who art in Heaven, Thy Kingdom come . . ."* (Matthew 6:9-13). This is meant to acknowledge the source of power, which is the Almighty.

Apart from faith, the Gospel of Prosperity as preached in the church emphasizes giving so that God will give one back in return. For Magaya, the prophet emphasises that if one gives little then God will give one little, as God looks at the value of our gift, the heart and motive of the giver.

Economic Message

A scholar on Pentecostalism, R. Okoko observes that when an individual or a society is deprived of certain basic things considered important such as education, food, nourishment, money, there are two religious doctrinal alternatives which can be invoked to overcome deprivation. These are (a) "The implementation of a doctrine in which some or all of these are considered meaningless or of low value could be adopted. (b) The implementation of religious doctrines through which these are considered important and can be acquired" (Akoko 2002: 368). Akoko postulates that the economic message of the Pentecostals revolves around the two alternatives. Our study indicates that PHD seems to have adopted the second alternative.

On the second approach, PHD ministries emphasises to believers that they can acquire possession of whatever they want on the basis of their faith. This faith is encouraged in the prosperity theology. This kind of theology teaches that the spiritual and material fortunes of a 'believer' are dependent on faith and on how much he gives spiritually and materially to God or his representatives (Marshall 1992: 2–32; Gifford 1991: 10–20). This implies that the riches of a 'believer' will be a consequence of his faith in God (Mk 11: 23, Deut. 20: 30, Phil. 4: 19, etc (Akoko 2002: 370).

Women's Participation in the Economy

A lot of PHD women who claim to have retreated from the social ills of life form the greatest number of attendees at church services, Their meeting days are Wednesday and Friday 5pm-8pm and Sunday 8am-5pm. Women are facing many problems which include domestic violence, rape cases, marriage problems where their husbands either cheat on them, leave them, do not support them with their children, or their in-laws hate them or they are single ladies, being bewitched, health problems such as barrenness, fibroids, menstrual complications, breast cancer, cervical cancer, HIV and AIDS, ulcers and economic problems which include poverty, limitation, failing businesses, unemployment and lack of promotion (Mundondo 2015: 45)

In terms of economic participation, PHD women have been and are involved in economic activities. Their faith in the Gospel of Prosperity encourages the members to engage in competitive business ventures on both a national and international levels. Most women get involved in small enterprises. According to one woman, Mrs T. Ncube, some women used to engage in cross border activities to order goods like basic commodities that have been in short supply during the times of inflation such as cooking oil, flour, sweets, beverages, clothing, car parts and accessories, blankets. But now (after 2009) that most of the items are available in shops in Harare, women prefer to trade in items such electrical gadgets that include TVs, fridges, irons, radios etc (Ncube interview 15/04/15)

Other women testified that they moved from one office to other selling snacks, house decoration items which they prepare, cosmetics, jewellery, etc. Some women also engaged in selling pots, plates and cups through joining some sales teams from South Africa. Some women in offices sell their items to colleagues from within their workplaces. A lot of PHD women are so enterprising such that they do not have restrictions on their own dressing and on the accumulation of wealth. They believe in fashion and nice appearances such that they dress gorgeously for church and put on elaborate hairstyles. There is a general Pentecostal church doctrine that believers can drive nice cars and own expensive foreign goods. Theirs is a strong belief that their ambition of accumulation is achieved and manifested in daily life, and is attributed to the goodness of God to God's people because of their faith. In that respect they maintain the maxim, *"Mbiri kuna Jesu"* (praise Jesus).

One woman said that she earned a living by cross border activities through selling second hand clothes and shoes packed in bales from Mozambique and Zambia. From this she was able to send her children to school, pay rentals and maintain a decent standard of living at home. She was the 'breadwinner' at home (Hove interview 15/04/15). The woman strongly believed in the power of God working in PHD Ministries. Another woman also testified that she was making her business flourish through her faith in PHD ministry's Gospel of Prosperity. She believed in the power of the anointing oil. According to her, she had been to Jerusalem and saw how the power of holy oil works. She also gave to God and the more she applied anointing oil, the more her business flourished. She said that she started her business with only $500 but within a month the money had tripled. In the end, she managed to buy a car. She has put PHD Ministries stickers all over her car as a testimony (Bizure interview 10/02/15).

A woman from PHD ministries testified in church that she had been retrenched from work for ten years. She tried to get re-engaged at work without success. In the end she sought legal action against the employer but without a solution. Her fortunes only turned positive when she approached the 'man of God,' Magaya. After a few days camp at the guest house, she received the blessings from the prophet that saw her regain her job. She had since opened a tuck shop where she sold basic commodities. She saluted the anointing which is bestowed upon the Prophet Magaya (Moyo 26/03/15). Other women were getting better paying jobs, as confirmed by one middle aged woman who testified that she wanted to be promoted to become the director of a company and she came to the 'Ladies Night' she 'seeded' with money as the prophet was preaching. The director just retired and left the position for her (Sakala interview 12/04/15). Some high fliers in PHD ministries have gone into business ventures that range from banking, printing, sale of Christian literature, tourism, and education, as well as the food industry which offer lucrative returns in contemporary Zimbabwe.

One church official, Talent Mango, said Magaya is famous for the construction of 420 houses for low income church workers. She said, "So far, Magaya has donated more than 10 houses to different people, and is unveiling a housing scheme for PHD Ministries' 1300 employees in Harare's Waterfalls suburb," (Mango interview 12/04/15). Most members confirmed that while Magaya had bought some land in Waterfalls to build a mega church, he was offered land by the government for the same purpose. Notably in PHD ministries, Magaya makes special preference for women to acquire land. His rationale is that most women have been marginalised by society. In that way the women's faith reaps the benefits of empowerment.

Magaya has also supported women's soccer by donating to Zimbabwe women's team, the Mighty Warriors. He gave each player a bottle of his popular anointing oil ahead of crunch Ghana match at Rufaro Stadium. And The Mighty Warriors hoped to overturn a 2-1 deficit. Magaya prayed for the girls during his Friday service. During the service, Magaya also pledged to donate money in the range of $US 28 0000 to offset ballooning ZIFA debt. (http://www.bulawayo24.com/index-id-news-sc-national-byo-65931.html, 10/05/15. That way Magaya has empowered women through sport.

From the above, women have embraced the advantages of the Gospel of prosperity which to them has produced some fruits. Many women have managed to earn a living, have become self sufficient and have also acquired other benefits that include good health, better paying jobs, get back their lost lovers, gotten married and made their businesses successful. To that extent some have managed to buy houses and own expensive cars through releasing their faith and using anointed oil They profess their faith in PHD ministries through open testimonies, stickers, online publicity, use of social media and print material. For them its *'mbiri kuna Jesu'* (glory to Jesus)for their success and prosperity.

Challenges faced by women

Although PHD ministries has enabled many women to engage in business, there are some challenges. One biggest challenge has been the criticisms of the gospel of prosperity. Most mainline churches dissuade their members from embracing the Pentecostal thrust on prosperity gospel. For them, salvation is attained by faith. Besides, they argue that the prosperity gospel has tended to enrich the rich and impoverished the poor (Sibanda interview 5/05/15).

Despite many testimonies of women testifying to have witnessed miracles and the hand of God through the gospel of prosperity, there are some devoted Christians in the church who have never received any miracle despite having all the faith, paying tithes and offerings, attending all church services, going to the guest house and using anointed items. So, quite a number have either slowed down in their participation, or have quit the church completely.

Giving and in particular the idea of seeding has raised serious controversies in PHD ministries. In one case the PH ministries founder Magaya was hit with a nearly $2 million lawsuit by an aggrieved Harare couple who allegedly pampered the man of the cloth with expensive vehicles and cash to fulfil a "prophecy" that they would own an airline. But since that did not materialise the matter was filed at the High Court in Harare on April 22 and 28 under case numbers HC36561/15, HC 3857/15 and 3858/15. Such claims tarnished Magaya's reputation.

Other people criticise Magaya's gospel of prosperity on the grounds that it is causing some women in the PHD Ministries to relax in terms of praying and doing productive work. Instead of putting faith in God, some women were putting all their faith and trust in the prophet, while others no longer prayed as they believe in the power of the anointed objects like oil, stickers and badges. The gospel also created pressure for prosperity such that some women abandoned their families in search of wealth and well being. This resulted in failing businesses, collapsing marriages and tension in families.

Some women, especially the youth and middle aged, were now pointing fingers at their families' old age as witches and wizards because of prophecy they are getting from the church. This gospel created a class of elite of women who believe are better than anyone else and do not want to be associated with those practising supernatural traditional religion.

There were clashes between Magaya and some members of the Apostolic Faith church. The war between Vapositori and PHD's leader Magaya started when he accused the Vapostori of using demonic powers. The war intensified when the Vapositori retaliated by claiming that they have approached its association for permission "to destroy artifacts" which they claim Magaya used to lure people to his church. The vapositori claimed that God had revealed to them that Magaya was not a Man of God, but used magic and other ungodly antics to lure people to his congregation. They said Magaya, who recently accused them of using evil spirits was the one who was possessed with demons and used evil spirits to lure people to his church. One of them said "Magaya has snakes that live in oil. The same oils are given to people as anointing oil. We want to destroy them. God has showed us (News Day 9/02/15)," This had a dent on the prophet Magaya's reputation.

In another case, Magaya invited a stripper-cum singer Beverly Sibanda' on the understanding that he would change her life after a transforming encounter with him. Magaya initially seemed to have convinced her to abandon her "dirty dancing" which was her source of livelihood on the grounds that the church was going to open a business for her, together with other young women eking out a living through stripping and sex work. Beverly immediately came to the church opposite Zindoga shopping centre in Waterfalls and agreed to quit her line of work and commit her life to God.

Other beneficiaries included Veronica Zhuwawo (28), who has been a dancer since she was 16, Mildred Chigaba (28), a stripper for seven years, Nomalanga Baureni (24), a prostitute and stripper together with Irene Masaka and Agnes Maringai, who too were ladies of the night. During the service, former Vahombe Queens dancer, Yvonne Javachava, gave a testimony of how she was delivered from dirty dancing and seducing men after receiving spiritual deliverance at PHD Ministries. Javachava said she would dance in a mini skirt to lure men as a way of survival and fending for her children since she was unemployed. She confessed that she would visit white garment apostolic churches to get love portions to lure men of which most of them would be married. "The first time I went to PHD Ministries I felt the power of God move in the congregation and I knew I had to change my lifestyle. I then bought a DVD and received a bottle of free anointing oil to use at home and the first time I took the oil, I vomited and knew that I was being delivered," (Javachava testimony 28/12/14). Observers noted that

PHD Ministries had become a hub for many local celebrities, with Madzibaba Nicholas Zacharia who has since become part of the praise team joining. Others who had been spotted in audiences include Douglas Chimbetu, Lawrence "Bhonzo" Simbarashe, Jesesi Mungoshi and Alick Macheso's wife, Nyaradzai (News Day 28/01/ 14). However whilst the women are hooked by the gospel of prosperity, most of them abandon the church after some of their aspirations do not come to fruituition. This has been the case with Bev in particular who has since left PHD ministries.

From the above, one can see that the gospel of prosperity is not working for some women. However, for others nothing has changed and some have persisted with the hope that one day all shall be well. Others have moved to other churches because they have lost all the hope and their faith has depreciated. Some people had looked at the prophet as their billow of hope but now due to scandals which he is being accused of, such as adultery, being a crowd puller who fights with others like Mapositori and the death of people at his crusade in Kwekwe, has resulted in other people doubting him. During this incident at Mbizo stadium in Kwekwe, four children and seven adults, including a pregnant woman, died during a stampede when an estimated crowd of 30 000 congregants attempted to leave the venue of a PHD Ministries service led by Magaya (News Day 22/11/14).

Conclusion

This paper chapter has provided insight into the changing shape of contemporary religion examining the new role that Pentecostal Christianity plays in the lives of young professional women who are enjoying career success and becoming part of Zimbabwe's new middle class. Notably, amongst these women an interesting relationship has emerged between work and religion to an extent that they feel that the social networks and self confidence they gain from their religious communities are as important as their spiritual experiences. It is clear that for some women, PHD ministries led by Magaya has offered new business opportunities and has provided theological justification for wealth creation and acquisition of new social status.

Sources

Interviews

Bizare interview 10/02/15

Hove S. interview 15/04/15

Mandizha interview 25.03/15

Maposa E. interview 10/04/15

Ncube T. interview 15/04/15

Moyo, N. 26/03/15.

Pambuka interview 25/03/15

Sakala interview 12/04/15

Shambare P. interview 30/03/15

Sibanda interview 5/05/15

References

Akoko R. M. "New Pentecostalism in the Wake Of The Economic Crisis In Cameroon," *Nordic Journal Of African Studies* 11(3), 2002, 359–376.

Biri, K. 'African Pentecostalism and Cultural Resilience: ZAOGA', Unpublished DPhil Thesis, Dept of Religious Studies, Harare: University of Zimbabwe, 2012.

Frahm-Arp, M. *Professional Women in South African Pentecostal Charismatic Churches*, Leiden: Brill, 2010.

Gbote, E.Z.M. and S.T.Kgatla, *Prosperity Gospel: A MissiologicalAssessment*, University of Pretoria, 2014.

Gifford, P. *The Religious Right in Southern Africa*, Harare, UZ, Publications, 1988.

Matenga, M. "TB Joshua dismisses 'dreaming' Magaya," *News Day* Zimbabwe, 10/04/14.

Mundondo, N. 'Gospel of Prosperity And Women In The Prophetic, Healing And Deliverance Ministries In Zimbabwe', Unpublished BA Hons Dissertation, Dept of Religious Studies, Harare: University of Zimbabwe, 2015.

Maxwell, D. 'Catch the Cockerel before Dawn: Pentecostalism and Politics in Post Colonial Zimbabwe', in*Africa*(LXX), / (2), 2000, pp.249–277.

Shoko, T. 'Independent Church Healing: The Case of St Elijah Cum Enlightenment School of the Holy Spirit in Zimbabwe'. *Studia Historiae Ecclesiasticae*, Vol XXX11 (3), Dec 2006, 130–153.

Shoko, T. 'Healing inHear the Word Ministries Pentecostal Church in Zimbabwe', in Westerlund D. (ed), *Global Pentecostalism*, London: I.B. Tauris Publishers, 2009, 43–55.

Sibanda, T. "Prophet Magaya to transform Bev's life" *News Day* 28/01/14 "Zimbabweans rush to Prophet Magaya of PHD ministries for miracle healing," ZimDiaspora,http://www.zimdiaspora.com/index.php?option=com_content&id=12347:many-prophet-magaya-of-phd-ministries-for-miracle-healing&Itemid=299, 29/07/13 Retrieved 1/05/15.

CHAPTER 8

Pentecostalism with Profits

An Exploration of Women-in-Entrepreneurship in ZAOGA (FIF) in Zimbabwe

RICHARD S. MAPOSA AND TAPIWA P. MAPURANGA

Introduction

PENTECOSTALISM IS NOT A new phenomenon in Christendom. It has roots that go back to the Pentecostal events of the last century and particularly goes back to the earliest corridors of church history itself. The long history of the Christian church is creamed with references to this Pentecostal phenomenon. For instance, the writings of the early church Fathers like Justin Martyr (100–165 AD), Tertullian (155–240 AD) and Origen (184–253 AD) are littered with the Pentecostal nuances. Even the great Reformers themselves attested to the reality of this Pentecostal phenomenon in their day, though some of them, because of the medieval superstition practices, condemned such Pentecostal dispositions.

Nevertheless, the historical rootage of modern Pentecostalism, relevant to the current study, is dated to 1st January 1901 when Miss Agness Ozman, a student at the Bethel Bible College, Kansas, USA was believed to have spoken in tongue at the laying of hands of the Principal, Charles Fox Parham (1873–1929). This single event and that was coupled with the Azusa Street revival spearheaded by the Apostolic Faith Mission in Los Angeles, USA launched Pentecostalism to global attention. Today, Pentecostalism is a brand of contemporary Christianity that is largely associated with the gospel of prosperity. It must be noted that the so-called prosperity gospel is the foundation of a surging theology of prosperity which advocates that people were and are created to be successful in life and enjoy full life in abundance (John 10:10). In fact, prosperity gospel deals with the health and well-being of people and works as a doctrine that financial blessing is part and parcel of the Will of God for true believers. Much of the inspiration is based on the Bible, specifically from the book of Malachi 3:7ff. The general conviction that ZAOGA FIF adherents uphold out of this gospel is that a person's faith in God who liberates, positive speech that believers can utter, donations and talents that believers undertake will all increase one's material wealth and well-being. Let us also be clearer here: The gospel of prosperity is understood efficaciously in the sense that it is a source of human empowerment in view of the fact that believers have a strong faith that God did not create people to suffer. ZAOGA (FIF) adherents are so powered by faith that promotes positive view of the spirit and body. The Bible is seen as a faith-document which provides a kind of a contract between God and believers (no longer people but believers set aside to control creation). God is faithful to the believers and believers themselves must work and powered by faith to fulfill Go's promises. Thus, the gospel of prosperity, when engaged in tandem with the working of talents in Pentecostal churches, like ZAOGA (FIF), and powered by faith, brings empowerment to people as individuals and as the church which exists like a "refugee camp" (Maxwell, 2006: 189). The popularity of this gospel of prosperity has in most instances emerged in times of economic turmoil. As such, members in various churches within Pentecostalism have managed to press on through the power of beliefs that shape this gospel of prosperity, which encourages them to push on, despite any economic challenges. Members are encouraged to get richer by the day, and shun away poverty. Women in Pentecostalism are no exception. A survey carried in most Pentecostal churches reveal that women are actually more active as entrepreneurs as compared to their male counterparts. Women are actively engaged in a variety of both micro and macro businesses which vary from selling vegetables, to owning larger businesses such as security companies, clothing retail shops, owning taxis among many other businesses. Accordingly, this is the context out of which we have perceived Pentecostalism to be a brand of Zimbabwean Christianity associated with socio-economic progress, especially when evaluated through the working of talents, both at the family and the church levels. Thus, it is the thrust of this chapter to explore how Pentecostalism has fuelled the practice of entrepreneurship amongst women with particular reference to Zimbabwe Assemblies of God Africa-Forward-in Faith (herein, ZAOGA-FIF) in Harare. Notwithstanding, we are convinced that the ZAOGA (FIF) women do represent what could be called "Pentecostalism-with-profits" in Zimbabwe.

[A]An Overview of Pentecostalism in Zimbabwe

The Zimbabwean religious landscape is hugely diverse (Taringa and Mapuranga 2010:37). Whilst some people have remained glued to African Traditional Religions, others have converted to world religions such as Islam, Christianity, Hinduism and the Baha'i Faith, amongst other religions. Though Zimbabwean Christianity is hugely diverse (Verstraelen 1998), this study will focus on one particular strand of Christianity: Pentecostalism. In the Zimbabwean context, Pentecostalism is not even a new phenomenon. In fact, the turn of the 19th century witnesses a great charismatic renewal which saw the birth of indigenous churches with a 'western touch' in terms of liturgy church conduct but anchored on unique soteriological beliefs. The emergence of Pentecostalism was largely facilitated by the Apostolic Faith Ministries which entered Zimbabwe in 1915 through an evangelist, Zacharias Manamela. Several schisms developed, leading to the formation of more Pentecostal churches within the Christian milieu in Zimbabwe. Thus, today, Pentecostalism represents the fastest growing brand of Christianity in Zimbabwe, if not the world over. Despite the allegations by secularization in relation to the decline in religiosity in Zimbabwe, there is the resurgence of religiosity and or unique spirituality evident in the Pentecostal tradition (Ndhlovu 2012:26). There is evidently a dynamic surge of Pentecostalism in Zimbabwe. As noted by Mapuranga (2012:116), "there is a transparent mushrooming of Pentecostal churches as compared to any other strands of Christianity, and other religions at large." Some of the most significant churches in Zimbabwean Pentecostalism today include the likes of Sprit Embassy, led by Eubert Angel, United Family International led by Emmanuel Makandiwa, Prophetic Healing and Deliverance Ministries led by Walter Magaya, amongst many others. However, these appear to be the newer forms of Pentecostalism in the Zimbabwean context. Originally, one would talk of Family of God led by Reverend Andrew Wutawunashe and Zimbabwe Assemblies of God led by Archbishop Ezekiel Guti, amongst a few others. Founded in 1960, ZAOGA (FIF) had arguably grown to be Zimbabwe's largest church, by the 1990s (Maxwell 1998). A common trait within all these Pentecostals is the notion of accumulating wealth and fighting against poverty and human impoverishment. As this study unfolds, we will examine the ways in which ZAOGA (FIF) has encouraged women to engage in various forms of businesses in order to raise wealth which makes life enjoyable. The economic activities of women in this particular church cannot be discussed adequately without drawing attention to their women's guild: Gracious Women.

ZAOGA (FIF)'s Gracious Women: A Brief Exploration

According to Mate (2002:553), Gracious Woman is a women's organization in ZAOGA (FIF) which was started in 1984 by Ezekiel Guti who, together with his wife, Eunor, started a prayer group for all women regardless of marital status is derived from the Bible. The Biblical basis for this women's group emerged from Proverbs 11:16 which reads, "A gracious woman is respected, but a woman without virtue is a disgrace." The group teaches women quite a number of issues which include marital, sexual, and fundraising ideas. As further argued by Mate (2002: 553), "to encourage women to participate in socio-economic development, thereby raising women's social standing," is one of the thrusts of the organization which becomes very critical for this study. Before we dwell on some of the projects embarked on by these women, we give an overview of the relationship between Pentecostalism and economic growth.

Pentecostalism and Economic growth: Friends or foes?

Earlier studies on Pentecostalism and the economy have noted symbiotic relationship between these two aspects (see for example Martin: 1990, Akoko: 2007, Musoni: 2013, Maxwell: 1998, 2005 & 2006, Ndhlovu 2012, amongst many others). According to Martin (1990: 205), there is a striking relationship between Pentecostalism and economic advancement. For him, these two aspects support each other. Without Pentecostalism, the economic culture within its adherents would not survive. In the same vein, without a vibrant economic culture, Pentecostalism too would not survive. Thus, Pentecostalism attracts converts because it combines material and spiritual improvement (Ndhlovu 2013: 44). This insight is instructive in view of the fact that a human being is made up of the body and the spirit. It makes sense because human life is not compartmentalized but a whole-holistic unity.

In most instances, this relationship emerges in situations where people have encountered poverty. In Zimbabwe, for example, the mushrooming of Pentecostalism was vibrant during the period beginning the early 2000s when inflation in Zimbabwe became very high and many people lost jobs. In a similar situation from Cameroon according to Akoko (2007:363):

> Another factor that accounts for the growth of the faith is the whole range of economic opportunities that have been opened up by these groups during this period of economic crisis affecting Cameroon. These Churches need a team of Pastors and other workers to work in their establishments. Many unemployed people have enrolled in Pentecostal Bible Colleges, not because of the pastoral call to serve but to earn a living. Some of the Churches have enormous projects and establishments such as schools, hospitals and banks. Employment opportunities are offered only to members of the Church and, as such, many people have joined in order to be employed.

As such, despite economic difficulties, Pentecostalism provides a shield for its followers in times of crisis. It becomes a place of refuge where believers who form a community find solace and help one another. It is in such light that Maxwell (1998) questions if indeed questions if Pentecostalism is delivering its adherents from the spirit of poverty. Furthermore, in a separate study, again, (Maxwell, 2006: 189) regarded the Pentecostal church to be like "refugee camp." This means that ZAOGA (FIF) exists as a transnational movement of people, though of different sociological make-up, but is solidly powered by a faith which knit believers together. This unique faith is works wonders for women's entrepreneurial initiatives in Zimbabwe. This is why the chapter traces the women's economic activities within the Harare scenario. With particular reference to ZAOGA FIF, Maxwell (2005) has pointed that in religion has become a "durawall of faith" during the crisis years after 2000, especially in the face of economic meltdown in Zimbabwe. This role of Pentecostalism in fighting poverty in Zimbabwe has also been noted by Ndhlovu (2013) who argues that in such instances where people hold on to their faith for economic survival, Pentecostalism becomes a form of protest movement against economic decline and tyranny. Whilst most of these studies tend to look at empowerment in general, this study concurs with Frahm Arp (2010) who examines how Pentecostal/Charismatic churches in South Africa have facilitated the upward mobility of women economically. One of the ZAOGA (FIF) pastors, Musoni

(2013:78) argues that there is a special focus of Pentecostalism on women. He says that women empowerment is a critical area where African Pentecostalism is central as a springboard of transforming society through the emancipation of women. With particular reference to ZAOGA FIF, Musoni (2013: 79) notes that:

> The women are taught to initiate various income generating projects. Some of the viable projects include, dress making, cross-border trading and vending. To a large extent, the study shows that many beneficiaries of the project have improved their lives, as individuals, families and societies at large. Today, for instance, most women in ZAOGA FIF driving their own brand new cars, they own magnificent houses, and they live modestly. This is sustainable development, when locals are economically empowered with pre-requisite tools for better life.

From the previous section, one would notice the obvious relationship between Pentecostalism and a vibrant economic culture in Harare, Zimbabwe. Pentecostalism has a unique way of addressing the economic needs of its adherents. As stated by Ndhlovu (2013: 45):

> The church's message of reformation qualifies it as a renewal movement that was aimed at protesting against economic decline and tyranny. . .Pentecostalism in Zimbabwe is a popular movement and grows very rapidly in conditions of economic decline and tyranny.

The next section details some of the ways in which women in ZAOGA FIF have been 'powered by their faith' to become active entrepreneurs in varying extents.

Women Entrepreneurial Activities in Harare

Women entrepreneurship in ZAOGA (FIF) represents a capitalist effort which is powered by an amazing human faith. From an insider's perspective of a Pentecostal faith system, patterns of entrepreneurship are understood to be part and parcel of the talents endowed in the individuals. The ZAOGA (FIF) theology of talents is critical in as far as appropriating the vitality of entrepreneurial activities at the backdrop of economic crisis in contemporary Zimbabwe. Firstly, it is valid that we identify the biblical foundations of talents and how they are conceived in ZAOGA (FIF). Secondly, we then highlight the scope of women entrepreneurship in Harare to determine how ZAOGA (FIF) as a brand of Pentecostal Christianity is contributing to the economic development that has great potentialities to transform the postcolonial Zimbabwean society.

Theology of Talents: Insider's Heartbeat

In the Collins English Dictionary, a talent is ordinarily defined as an innate ability, aptitude or faculty. Some simple examples are: the talent of cooking, gardening and marketing. From a Pentecostal believer's standpoint, a talent is designed by God to uplift the physical and spiritual living standards of a person = believer (a true believer is one who can always speak in tongues!). Phenomenologically speaking, a talent is described by the ZAOGA (FIF) believer as *tarenda* (singular) or *matarenda* (plural). Talents are done by both men and women of every sociological profile and age. *Tarenda* generally understood to be money got from using hands, especially by selling things. There are two main forms of *matarenda* in ZAOGA (FIF) Church. One, there are *matarenda emudzimba* (home talents). Home talents are done mostly by women and used to uplift the family. Women usually end up buying items meant to renew the kitchen or the bedroom and also clothes for the family. Two, there are also the ordinary talents meant for the church upkeep and used to embark on the projects. True believers do not need to use this kind of money but give it to embark and sustain ZAOGA (FIF) Church projects like building clinics and hospitals (for instance, Mbuya Dorcus Hospital in Waterfalls suburb, Harare), schools (for instance, Grange Christian School), university (like, Zimbabwe Ezekiel Guti University in Bindura). When a believer works talents to a certain target, that is, a certain amount of money, one is given a certificate of success. Talents possess extrinsic value because almost all our informants for the study concurred that the essence of talents is to encourage people to work hard so that people can enjoy life in abundance (John 10:10). We also decoded the fact that talents are linked to people's relationship to God to the extent that true believers actually sing some songs to show their sense of spiritual edification. One interviewee had the audacity to simplistically sing to demonstarate the meaning and ethos of talents, thus:

> *Talenta chikoro chatakapuwa nababa Guti.matalenta anotsvaira urombo achiunza nyasha.Tino bata matarenda nemaoko.*

> "Talents constitute a form of school bestowed to us by Archbishop Guti. Talents erase poverty. We work talents using hands."

Drawn from the song above, it must be noted that the theological motivation is that every true believer should be encouraged to work using together one's hands and brains as prescribed and ordained at the point of human creation by God. The biblical inspiration is firstly found in the book of Genesis. For instance, in the fall of man (also woman therein by implication) in the Garden of Eden (Genesis 3:17), man was told to work hard in order to eat and sustain for one's life. In the book of Proverbs 31:10ff) where a woman is encouraged to work to please the husband all the days of her life. In the New Testament, the theology of talents is derived from the parable of Talents (Matthew 25:14ff; Luke 19:12ff).

The Archbishop Ezekiel Handinawangu Guti in his book, *History of ZAOGA, Forward in Faith* (1999:48ff) mentions how the theology of talents intrinsically evolved and intertwined with the history of ZAOGA (FIF). Guti recalled the episode in the USA when he was offered money by a white man to establish a church. The story claimed that Ezekiel Guti rejected the offer because God told him that people themselves should learn to use their own hands working meaningful talents that are commensurate with the individual's specific skills and capabilities so as to be self-reliant and sustain one's life efficaciously. Guti then approached one woman, Priscilla Ngoma, to initially guide the working of talents in ZAOGA (FIF) as an indigenous religious movement in Zimbabwe (Simango, 2012, 11).

This theology of talents is meant to propel pastoral ministry and also provide basic vocational pedagogy to the church members to earn a living and not to be dependent on others like mere children. In the context of the study, it is prudent to point out that the fundamental nature of the talents provides a window for entrepreneurial empowerment and also captures the essence of the Zimbabwe Agenda for Sustainable Socio-Economic Transformation (herein, ZIM ASSET) as a national indigenization policy for societal transformation in contemporary Zimbabwe. The baseline is that the theology of talents efficaciously affects the basic lives of the people towards change. The redemptive law of working talents is that if a person gives, one receives, if one works, then one gets an earning and thereto enjoys living. Thus, from the ZAOGA (FIF) insider's standpoint, a talent is both a benevolent fund-raising and fund-generating project manifesting God's blessing which comes as an endowed gift to an individual (Durran, 2003:13). The underlying conviction is that God blesses a diligent worker to become victorious and not victims of any existential circumstances or situations (Deuteronomy 8:18ff). As much as we can say, the theology of talents is inclusively connected to the 'fifth' gospel of prosperity which is arousing shockwaves in almost all the Pentecostal churches in contemporary Zimbabwe. Why shockwaves? Inspired from the command of Malachi (3:7–11) it must be underscored that the working of talents, literally, constitutes the goose that can hatch the golden eggs towards prosperity. In simple terms, we are saying that working talents is a way of empowering the economically marginalized people. In addition, the working of talents provides a 'deliverance school' as a way-out from poverty and marginalization. Moreover, there is neither age limit nor social class in the working of talents because ever person is perceived to be divinely endowed with a particularistic innate skill or skills which mainstream society should benefit from. Nevertheless, the system of working talents in ZAOGA (FIF) is not without criticisms. Among others, ZAOGA (FIF) is usually disparaged for masquerading as a transnational profit-making organization whose capitalist ethic is indicted of ripping off its members of money and neglecting the primary pastoral role to concentrate on economic businesses which is the domain of corporate organizations. This is how ZAOGA (FIF) appears to be concentrating on the prosperity gospel that sells God at the market at the expense of the anticipated human eternity. It is on the basis of these insights that we reflect on some patterns of micro economic activities that women in ZAOGA (FIF) are involved in Harare. Some three patterns of micro entrepreneurial activities below speak volumes for themselves within the ZAOGA (FIF) women fraternity in Harare.

Dynamics of Entrepreneurship

First and foremost, women are significantly involved in money dealing through money clubs. The money clubs constitute a ubiquitous contribution for women's entrepreneurship within the church in the context of Harare. Money club as micro entrepreneurial business was widened and deepened in scope more because of the economic challenges. In almost every ZAOGA (FIF) Church assembly in Harare, women organize themselves around the money clubs as a pivotal survival strategy at a time the country is facing economic conundrum. The study observed that every money club is administered by women themselves on sound accounting principles. For example, in each money club, there is elected leaderships, books of accounts, borrowing system, banking and disciplinary system, among others. What happens is that every month each member contributes pool money according to one's capacity or capability. For instance, in one model money club of fifteen members, members contribute money ranging from $100-00 to $500-00 a month. In terms of sociological profile, members are drawn, literally from all walks of life. The women do not discriminate each other on account of social class, level of education, profession jobs and the like. Rather, those women gather together to work for the Kingdom of God under the auspices of the talents and the love to uplift or improve the status of their families in some fundamental ways. For instance, when they share the profits, these women always use 40% of the profits to buy items of their choice that help to re-furnish their kitchens or the alternatively bedrooms.

Secondly, today's women in ZAOGA (FIF) Church have a stake in micro business through the establishment of tuck shops within Harare. There are strings of tuck shops that belong to or owned by women in every residential place and location in Harare. The tuck shops represent a thriving small-to-medium grocery business where ZAOGA (FIF) women participate with great zeal and powered by astonishing human faith. In the recent times, the tuck shops have emerged with rapidity as poor urbanites literally grabbed the peri-urban farms to open new human settlements for themselves in the fashion that resembled how the poor rural people grabbed the white commercial farms for black occupation after 2000. Accordingly, the City of Harare witnessed the sprawling of new formal and informal residential areas like Hopley, Retreat, Stoneridge, Dumfalls, Ruwa, Timire, among others. Yet, the common characteristic features of these new settlements are that, among others: no properly structured social services like shops, schools and health facilities. Thus, some ZAOGA (FIF) women organized themselves to fill in the gap by establishing a string of tuck shops. The tuck shops are organized more on cooperative and capitalist lines. For instance, in April 2013, four women opened a tuck shop in Retreat area. Three other women opened a tuck shop in Stoneridge in August 2014. We are more interested in illustrating the organizational model of women-in tuck shops in Stoneridge. The three women allocated each a special responsibility according to one's skills, talents and professional attributes. The first woman who is a stay-at-home person is responsible for selling the goods as a tuck shop keeper. The second woman who is a school teacher functions as an auditor. The third and last woman who owns a small car is normally responsible for some tuck shop orders from Mbare Musika, among other places. These women share the money (profits) three times: in April, August and December of every year. In terms of impact to their families, these women testified that their contribution to both the quantity and quality of the disposal income was great and far reaching to transform lives.

Thirdly, a number of ZAOGA (FIF) women participate in the cross-border syndicates. In this entrepreneurship, most women go to popular African destinations like South Africa, Botswana, Mozambique, Zambia and Malawi to bring well-liked goods for re-trade that range from groceries, cloths to kitchenware. Beyond the African region, women ply to such far away East Look places like Dubai, Malaysia and China. One notable feature of women who go beyond Africa is that they are people of great material means in society. Some ZAOGA (FIF) women are money sharks, since they are spouses of great men of high society who function as captains of industry and commerce in Zimbabwe. These rich men allow their wives to be in touch with other fellow church women to advance the Christian spirit of *agape* which is best exemplified through the praxis of human fellowship and solidarity with the common person (woman) in society. Some of the wealthier women who are involved in this cross border trade are the ones who own ostentatious flea markets, hair saloons, barbershops, garment outlets, Eco Cash booths, foreign currency aisles and flower boutiques in the upmarket zones of the Central Business District (CBD) of Harare.

Challenges Associated with Women Entrepreneurship

Despite the forwarding-looking entrepreneurship in ZAOGA (FIF) Church, women still experience a host of challenges associated their work in Harare. Some four decisivechallenges are cited in this section, thus:

First, gender relations continue to be a sticky issue that militates against women's micro economic entrepreneurship. The cultural system of patriarchy still reigns over society in Zimbabwe despite modernity or globalization. This explains why a few women have the liberty to visit foreign places like Dubai or Malaysia as married women are coerced not to do so by their husbands. Second,most of the women's church-related economic initiatives lack public funding in view of the fact that the clubs are not registered with the Office of the Registrar, neither at the ministerial level within the Government of Zimbabwe. Third, most of the members do not have the much-needed technical know-how to run the entrepreneurial clubs on sound cooperative basis due to lack of proper formal education. Their initiatives are simply powered by faith. Women lack proper vocational training. Four, most of the women interviewed for this study pointed out the challenge of economic sanctions currently reeling Zimbabwe. Women said that majority of Zimbabweans; people who constitute market have no cash in their hands to buy products at the market. Industries are downsizing their workforce. Today there is mass unemployment in the country and many people are cashless vendors in the streets of Harare. Despite these challenges, the ZAOGA (FIF) women are powered by great faith and determination in participating in the informal sector to transform their lives as individuals and families in postcolonial Zimbabwe. It is faith fired inspired by God that propel them to soldier on at the backdrop of the informal sector that to them, has become the formal sector. Like the power of the wisdom of the Ecclesiastes (3:1ff), women in ZAOGA (FIF) believe that there is time for everything purpose under heaven. Evidently, the working of talents is a crucial survival strategy meant to regenerate lives and society, especially judged in the context of the economic crisis in contemporary Zimbabwe.

Concluding Remarks

The study made it evident that in a number of critical ways women entrepreneurship is vital to revive the national economy. Contemporary Zimbabwe is a country that is going through a number of challenges. Nevertheless, the study outlined, described and explained the multifarious ways in which ZAOGA (FIF) women who are powered by faith, are making economic strides to improve themselves and their families. Women's initiatives provide a window to gauge what reconstruction theology can do in the Zimbabwean context. From a feminist theological perspective, economic entrepreneurship is a redemptive route that empowers humanity and helps women to be self-reliant. It was also shown that the patterns and dynamics of women's contributions increase the quality and quantity of disposable incomes to their families in loaded ways. In this manner, the ZAOGA (FIF) women's entrepreneurship carries some anecdotes underscoring the sanctity of human redemption and transformation in society. We wish to conclude this discourse by making a theological insight: every micro enterprise is a mind-set helpful to restore the divine original Order of Creation and has great potentialities to level the gaps embedded in the gender masculinities in the Zimbabwean society that is currently smarting from cross-cultural indentation and neo-colonialism, largely on account of globalization today.

References

Akoko, R. M. (2007). *Ask and you will be given: Pentecostalism and the economic crisis in Cameroon.* Leiden: African Studies.

Chitando, E (2013), "Prophets, Profits and Protests: Prosperity Theology and Zimbabwean Gospel Music," in Ezra Chitando, Masiiwa Ragies Gunda and Joachim Kugler (eds.), *Prophets, Profits and the Bible in Zimbabwe,* University of Bamberg Press: Bamberg.

Durran, M. *Fundraising for Churches,* London: Canterbury Press, 2003.

Frahm- Arp, M, (2010),*Professionalwomen in South African Pentecostal Charismatic churches,* Leiden: Brill

Guti, E.H. *History of ZAOGA, Forward in Faith,* Harare: EGEA Publications, 1999.

Guti, E.H. *The Church and Political Responsibility,* Harare: EGEA Publications, 1994.

Mapuranga T.P (2012). "Youth and the culture of Pentecostalism as a Survival Strategy for Female Students at the University of Zimbabwe, 2000-2008," in Space Transformation and Representation: Reflections on University Culture, Olatunde Bayo Lawuyi and Chinyere Ukpokolo (eds.), New Jersey: Goldline and Jacobs Publishers, 109-122.

Mate, R., (2002). "Wombs as God's Laboratories: Pentecostal Discourses of Femininity in Zimbabwe," in *Africa: Journal of the International African Institute,*Vol.72 (4), 549-568.

Maxwell, D. (2006). *African Gifts of the Spirit: The Rise of a Zimbabwean based Transnational Religious Movement,* Oxford, James Carrey.

Maxwell, D. (2005). The Durawall of Faith: Pentecostal Spirituality in neo-Liberal Zimbabwe, *Journal of Religion in Africa,* 35, no 14-32.

Maxwell, D. (1998). "'Delivered from the Spirit of Poverty': Pentecostalism, Prosperity and Modernity in Zimbabwe," *Journal of Religion in Africa 28(4),* 350-373.

Musoni, P. (2013) "African Pentecostalism and Sustainable Development: A Study of Zimbabwe Assemblies of God Africa Forward in Faith Church," in *International Journal of Humanities and Social Science Invention,* Vol. 2 (10), 75-82.

Ndlovu, Lovemore. (2012). "Pentecostalism as a Form of Protest Movement against Economic Decline and Tyranny: The Case of Celebration Church in Zimbabwe," *Serbian Political Thought 5(1),* 25-47.

Nogueira-Godsey, T., (2012). "Weberian Sociology and the Study of Pentecostalism: Historical Patterns and Prospects for the Future," *Journal for the Study of Religion,* Vol. 25, (2,) 51-69.

Simango, J. 'ZAOGA (FIF)'s Story in Fundraising: Assessing the Impact of Working Talents for God's Purpose and Organizational Development at Hatfield District', Diploma Project Submitted at Africa Leading Development Network, Harare; June 2012.

Taringa, N.T and Mapuranga, T.P (2010), "Pluralism and Islam: A historical and Sociological Analysis." in, *Faith in the City: the Role and Place of Religion in Harare,* L Togarasei and E Chitando (eds.), Uppsala: Swedish Science Press. 137-152.

Togarasei, Lovemore. (2010). "Churches for the Rich? Pentecostalism and Elitism," in Lovemore Togarasei and Ezra Chitando, eds., *Faith in the City: The Role and Place of Religion in Harare*. Uppsala: Swedish Science Pr.

Verstraelen, F.J (1998), *Zimbabwean Realities and Christian Responses*, Gweru: Mambo Press.

CHAPTER 9

Conclusion
Patterns in Pentecostal Women in Business
A Theoretical Exploration of Pentecostalism and Economic Culture in Zimbabwe

TAPIWA PRAISE MAPURANGA

Introduction

THE CHAPTERS THAT HAVE been presented from this study generally illustrate that the rise in Pentecostalism has seen the empowerment of most people economically and financially. According to Mate (2002:549), "economically a small but growing number of black families have experienced some upward mobility-something these Churches encourage through 'the gospel of prosperity." This study will explore the relationship between Pentecostalism and economic growth in Zimbabwe. This chapter's distinctive contribution to the emerging body of knowledge on Pentecostalism in Zimbabwe can be located in its emphasis on the extent to which Pentecostalism has facilitated the growth of economically independent women. Although earlier authors had emphasised the point that Pentecostalism grants women greater leadership space for women (see Mapuranga 2013), the area of women's economic emancipation in the majority of ministries within the Pentecostal fraternity appears to have escaped scholarly scrutiny. This chapter plugs this gap in the scholarly literature by highlighting the extent to Pentecostalism has created an ethic for the creation and control of the finances and economy for women. These ministries have helped them built their own niche and become financially independent. Through Pentecostalism, they now exercise their own agency within that space. One would agree that Pentecostalism has the potential to ensure that women enjoy "living with dignity," in finances (Mouton *et al* 2015). This study thus argues that Pentecostalism has a unique way of empowering its adherents and rescuing them from poverty.

Methodologically, this research basically utilise textual analysis. It examines the validity and applicability of theories proposed by selected sociologists of religion over the years. Apart from the texts, this study also substantiates its arguments through information gathered over 8 years (from 2008 to 2015) during which the researcher has been actively involved in researching on Pentecostalism and gender in Zimbabwe. This information has been gathered through testimonies, sermonic discourses and interviews from female Pentecostals. These will be used to make a link between theories of Pentecostalism and economic culture. The next section gives an overview of the theories that propose a relationship between religion (in this case; Pentecostalism) and financial development.

Revisiting earlier Theories on Religion and Development

According to Max Weber (1930, 1958), "The Protestant ethic gave rise to the spirit of capitalism." Weber attributed the success of mass production largely to the Protestant ethic. Despite the criticisms against his theory, Weber's ideas became a stepping stone to a lot more theories that have emerged over the years on the relationship between religion and capitalism. Apart from Weber, more recent scholars have attempted to find the link between religion, particularly Pentecostalism and culture (see for example, Peter Berger (1967, 2004), Redding (1990), Martin (1990, 2002), and Miller and Yamamori (2007 amongst others). Peter Berger developed a theory that directly speaks to Pentecostalism and its relationship to economic development. He called it the Pentecostal ethic for development and the trend recognises Pentecostals as possessing an equivalent to what Weber described as an ethic of inner-worldly asceticism (Nogueira-Godsey 2012:55). Redding's research culminated in a book entitled, *The Spirit of Chinese Capitalism* (1990), and Martin researched on Pentecostalism in Latin America that resulted in the book, *Tongues of Fire* (1990).The largest application of Peter Berger's Pentecostal ethic for Development was carried out in South

Africa in 2008 by the Centre of Development and Enterprise, culminating in the publication, "Under the Radar: Pentecostalism in South Africa and Its Potential Social and Economic Role" (Nogueira-Godsey 2012:60).

Consequently, this chapter argues that such theories can be applied to the current wave of Pentecostalism in Africa, with particular reference to Zimbabwe. According to Miller and Yamamori (2007:164), the "lifestyle of Pentecostals does not differ substantially from Weber's description of the Puritans." Despite the criticisms that have been levelled against the applicability of these theories (Coleman 1968, Stokes 1975, Brusco 2009, and more recently, Nogueira-Godsey 2012), this chapter, and indeed this whole publication, still argues that there is a Pentecostal ethic which is largely responsible for the increased entrepreneurship amongst its women believers.

The next section who explore the relationship Pentecostalism and its ability to 'deliver people from the spirit of poverty' (Maxwell 1998) in Zimbabwe.

The Rise of Pentecostalism and the Crisis Period: A Brief Analysis

The influence of Pentecostalism and its gospel of prosperity began to have a greater effect, especially on women, during the crisis period which began around the 2000s in Zimbabwe. More ministries emerged during this period of massive financial endurance by the majority of Zimbabweans. This study concurs with Akoko (2007) who argues that the increase in Pentecostalism and its unique way of addressing the economic needs of its adherents partly led to the increase of these Pentecostal ministries. According to Akoko (2007: 360), with particular reference to Cameroon:

> The rise and spread of Pentecostalism during this period of the crisis - as in many other parts in Africa - coupled with mass defections from the established churches to the new churches – could be interpreted as a public sign of dissatisfaction by Christians with the way the established churches have gone about addressing the spiritual and material needs of their followers. Such increasing disillusionment shows that a swelling number of Christians do not consider it enough for the churches simply to make critical statements about the worsening economic situation or condemning the few who live in obscene opulence while the majority wallow in misery and poverty.

What Akoko notes with reference to Cameroon can be equally applied to the Zimbabwean scenario. Many people continue to join Pentecostal churches because they feel that the new religion will cushion them from economic turmoil. As is noted by Akoko about Cameroon, Pentecostalism has brought many employment opportunities and self-help projects. He argues(2007:363):

> Another factor that accounts for the growth of the faith is the whole range of economic opportunities that have been opened up by these groups during this period of economic crisis affecting Cameroon. These Churches need a team of Pastors and other workers to work in their establishments. Many unemployed people have enrolled in Pentecostal Bible Colleges, not because of the pastoral call to serve but to earn a living. Some of the Churches have enormous projects and establishments such as schools, hospitals and banks. Employment opportunities are offered only to members of the Church and, as such, many people have joined in order to be employed.

This study agrees with Zimunya and Gwara (2013:191) who argue that:

> In this scenario of turbulent and uncertain events, Pentecostal churches have sprouted and offered a much needed solace... The influx of new membership to Pentecostal Church Ministries has continued to swell due to the fact that many people have through Pentecostalism had their physical and spiritual problems supposedly solved and have also claimed to discover the root causes of generational curses which run through their ancestral lineages.

From the aforementioned, this study concludes that Pentecostalism has a peculiar ethic that transforms the lives of women from 'grass to grace' (as some Pentecostal preachers express it). Maxwell (1998) thus questions if Pentecostalism is in real essence 'delivering people from the spirit of poverty'. Essentially, the study argues that women's lives are being transformed for the better from poverty to prosperity. It will highlight some of the ways in which Pentecostal beliefs relating to hard work have transformed the lives of women in particular. But first, the next section briefly highlights how this transformation from poverty to prosperity is highly related to the gospel of prosperity in Pentecostalism.

Conversion to Pentecostalism: creating a different person

This chapter concurs with earlier studies which suggest that the moment one converts to Pentecostalism or becomes 'born again' there is a way in which they become resocialised to become new people, who should fit into the 'born again, as this guarantees one to 'make a complete break with the past and get providence' (Marshall 2010:204). Martin (1990:287) describes this as a 'revision of consciousness'. Amongst other new and better characteristics that the new believer adopts, Maxwell (1998: 353–54) mentions traits that are important for this study: economic attributes. For him, "the re-socialisation makes the born-again believer more industrious and socially mobile than many of their 'unsaved' neighbours..." The relationship between Pentecostalism and a positive change in one's economic status can be attributed to the increased attendance in the churches. For Chitando (2013:99), prosperity theology became therefore, a 'faith with Profits'. This justifies the argument by Bourdillon (1993:85) that "the package of a religion affects people's choice of it." According to Togarasei (2010:26), "Pentecostalism has been packaged to meet the needs and aspirations" of its followers. Pentecostalism in Zimbabwe has ways through which it informs its adherents to seek economic transformation. Like Berger (2004) in his studies on Latin America, this particular study highlights and relates a peculiar Pentecostal ethic to the economic survival of women in Pentecostal churches. Chief amongst these traits is the adherents to the gospel of prosperity within Pentecostalism.

The gospel of prosperity and the ethic of entrepreneurship

One of the key tenets of Pentecostal theology is the gospel of prosperity. According to Asamoah (2013:198):

> Prosperity theology, sometimes referred to as the prosperity gospel, the health and wealth gospel, or the gospel of success is a Christian religious doctrine that financial blessing is the will of God for Christians, and that faith, positive speech, and donations to Christian ministries will always increase one's material wealth.

The next section tries to come up with possible explanations as to how the gospel of prosperity creates one's capability to be an entrepreneur; even in the slightest sense (what Martin 1990:206 calls penny capitalism).

Gifford (1988), Ayegboyin (2011) and Garrard-Burnett (2012) are some of the scholars who have explained prosperity theology as a specifically Pentecostal doctrine that places emphasis on the attainment of wealth and health in the life before death. For Gifford for example, its origins were from the biblical text of Matthew 11:23ff. The basic teaching is that God wants the Christian to be wealthy and that poverty is an indication of personal sin. A further tenet, based on a tendentious reading of 2 Corinthians 9 is that in order to reap, one must sow. This means that the Christian must contribute abundantly to the work of evangelism and to the upkeep of his/her Pastors, if he/she wishes health and material wealth themselves.

Alongside Gifford's observation, Mate (2002) maintains that Pentecostalism provides an ideological framework which legitimises behaviours contrary to tradition. They encourage individualism, which not only enables saving and accumulation, but also a process of class

formation. In the faith Gospel, personal testimony sometimes occupies an even more important place than the Bible itself. In these organisations, laziness and poverty are attributed to the work of the devil, who is inimical to productivity. Generosity of giving, 'conspicuous charity' to the Church (also referred to as 'planting'), enables Church founders and those close to them to live lavish life styles, drive expensive cars and support 'conspicuous consumption'. Church members create a prosperous Church: it is like a high-yielding investment in God. The 'gospel of prosperity' becomes a way of attracting membership and retaining it, especially among the poor aspiring to break out of their poverty.

These ideas by Gifford and Mate are further reiterated by Chitando (2013:99) who argues that "the major characteristic of prosperity theology is the idea that success in life's endeavours is an integral part of a Christian's experience of salvation. Salvation is not an event to be experienced in the remote future: it is a present possibility and reality."

The gospel of prosperity creates an ethic for its believers to strive to be prosperous. According to Togarasei (2005: 370), "the poor in the church see themselves as upwardly mobile. The theology of prosperity makes them feel that they are in the process of transformation to a higher status in life, and they are convinced that Jesus Christ will deliver them from poverty."

This is supported by Maxwell (2006:204) who argues that:

> Zimbabwean Pentecostal churches stress the view that God gave human beings dominion over the world, and human beings are now responsible for realising their dreams by creating wealth

through gifts and tithing in the church. On the basis of Malachi 3:10, people are taught that the more they give the more they will receive from God, who will open the windows of heaven and shower upon them heavenly blessings in the form of money and other possessions. The "born again" are urged to reject their ancestral spirits on the understanding that they are responsible for the poverty of Zimbabweans.

However, the theology of prosperity has been met with different perspectives on how it transforms the lives of its adherents economically. On the one hand, scholars like James Amanze (2008: 7) argue that it is largely "exploiting the masses." He argues that:

> It has been observed in many quarters that the theology of prosperity is anything but helpful to people, and in fact exploits human frailties such as disease, the fear of death, and suffering in general. A related criticism is that the gospel of prosperity exploits the poor, as it is claimed that in some instances the tithes of the poor support a pastor in maintaining a lavish lifestyle. (In this context, the example of the late Archbishop Benson Idahosa in Benin, Nigeria, is cited.) It is reported that in some of the new Pentecostal Churches in Ghana, members are sometimes urged to borrow money, if necessary, in order to give to the church. They are told that by doing so, they qualify for supernatural monetary blessing. This, I contend, is an abuse of the system of giving and tithing in the Church and a form of exploitation of human beings by other human beings.

On the other hand, Pentecostalism and its gospel of prosperity is indeed transforming the lives of its adherents. According to Akoko (2007: 5) there is the contention that:

> God has mercifully provided for all the needs of humanity in the suffering and death of Christ, and every Christian should now share the victory of Christ over sickness and poverty. A believer has a right to the blessing of health and wealth won by Christ. He or she can obtain these blessings merely by emphatic confession of faith. The spiritual and material fortunes of a believer depend on faith and on how much the believer gives spiritually and materially to God or his representative in the world. Great emphasis is placed on the importance of financial prosperity and financial giving here and now. People are encouraged to pay "seed money" to the church as a means of generating wealth. As the slogan goes, "you

prosper by planting a financial seed in faith, the return on which will meet all your financial needs."

From the aforementioned, one might conclude that the gospel of prosperity is highly responsible for endorsing the ideology that inspires women to thrive and make their money.

Maria Frahm-Arp (2010) also identifies this as among four elements that stand as central themes that help to empower women, in her case, 'professional women in South African Charismatic churches.' These four elements are (i) the gospel of prosperity, (ii) stewardship, (iii) integrity and (iv) balance of work and family. These elements that drive women in South African Pentecostalism can be compared to the Zimbabwean case. In the next section, this study turns to these other tenets that create this Pentecostal ethic of entrepreneurship.

The role of stewardship, integrity and balance of work and family

Frahm-Arp, apart from the gospel of prosperity also identifies 'stewardship' (2010: 177). This element is also reinforced in Pentecostalism as women are taught to be responsible in their management of resources and time. In an interview, Ms Mutezo (2014) from the Prophetic, Healing and Deliverance (PHD) Ministry raised this point. She indicated that the teachings of her prophet on the wise management of time so that they are able to maximise the use of time. This is designed so that they can make more profits in business. This is in agreement with Frahm-Arp's study on South African women on the significance of the teachings of stewardship as a unique Pentecostal ethic that empowers women in becoming more economically capacitated.

Furthermore, the element that stands out as a central theme in Pentecostalism in financially empowering women is the 'exhortation to do all things with integrity and not capitulate into bribery' (Frahm-Arp 2010: 177). Such teachings are biblical, stemming from verses such as Isaiah 33: 15 where righteousness is exalted. Women are taught critical values in business and this breeds a fertile ground for making clean profits with integrity.

Last but not least, this study concurs with Frahm-Arp that Pentecostalism provides a strong foundation for the breeding ground for money making for women through the fourth element that 'encourages balance between work and family' (Frahm-Arp 2010: 178). Women are encouraged to play their roles as mothers and providers for their families. For example,

Mate (2002:564) notes that Precious Stones, a Pentecostal women's group, view motherhood as important 'work of God' and an 'altar of sacrifice' and liken it to Mary's role in the birth of Jesus Christ. Dr Wutaunashe, the founder, says that at this altar women offer their bodies (wombs) for God's work as 'God's laboratory' out of which 'miracles are produced' (Mate 2002). Thus, no matter how women toil to look for money, they should have a balance between their businesses and their families as an illustration of their value for motherhood.

From the above assertions, this study notes that Pentecostalism enables the society, women in particular, to adjust from poverty through some of the doctrines outlined above. This movement has ways through which it helps its members to live within the demands of a particular situation. According to Maxwell (1998:351), Pentecostalism:

> explains the prevalence of the doctrines not in terms of false consciousness or right wing conspiracy but as means of enabling Pentecostals to make the best of rapid social change. For some, the doctrines have engendered social mobility. For others, they provide a code of conduct which guards them from falling into poverty and destitution. For all they provide a pattern of coming to terms with, and benefiting from, modernity's dominant values and institutions.

Having explored the significance of some doctrines that provide an enabling environment for the production of wealth, the next section gives some highlights on what exactly has occurred from selected examples in Zimbabwean Pentecostalism.

Insights from Zimbabwean Pentecostalism

Zimbabwean women have always been quite active in informal businesses. With phases of financial challenges in the Zimbabwean economy such as the Economic Structural Adjustment Programme in the 1990s, women had since started to become important players with the responsibility of securing finances in the home. They were involved in activities such as selling fruit and vegetables, clothes, crafts, amongst others (see Mupedziswa and Gumbo 2001:30). Bearing this in mind, this chapter argues that the coming on board of a new wave of Pentecostalism (particularly from the 2000s), more women became increasingly motivated by the aforementioned Pentecostal ethic to remain astute in the various business to sustain their families, despite the tough economy. Whilst the previous section generally highlights the critical Pentecostal ethic that 'powers women by faith' to become successful businesswomen and entrepreneurs, this section provides particular insights from Zimbabwean Pentecostalism.

The examples of prominent women's groups in Zimbabwean Pentecostalism are: the Gracious Woman of the Zimbabwe Assemblies of God (ZAOGA) and the Precious Stones from Family of God (FOG). These were the earliest known women's ministries that were known to encourage and support women's financial endeavours. However, this study concurs with Ndhlovu (2012) that newer churches began to emerge in response to socio-economic challenges. Hence, one finds a plethora of other mushrooming ministries within Zimbabwean Pentecostalism.

Gracious Woman of the Zimbabwe Assemblies of God (ZAOGA)

To start with, ZAOGA is well known for empowering women through a variety of its programmes and projects through the women's organisation called the Gracious Woman. According to Mate (2002:553), Gracious Woman is derived from the Bible, Proverbs 11:16, which reads, "A gracious woman is respected, but a woman without virtue is a disgrace." A key identity marker of a Gracious Woman is working hard. Mrs Murwira (2015), a member of Gracious Woman, noted that, "Being a wise woman also involves working hard as we are taught by Mai Guti." Mrs Guti is the wife of Ezekiel Guti, the founder of ZAOGA. Critical to this group are projects such as "talents" (money which one is given from church and one needs to return it in two fold or more), "round tables" (here women put themselves into groups that borrow money from each other and return the money with interest) (see also Biri 2012:51–52). Women are encouraged to work hard and supplement the income of their husbands. The general consensus being that a wise woman should work hard to sustain the family. Musoni (2013:78–79) argues that the talents are made to uplift the status of women through engaging in self reliance jobs. This is taken from the parable of the talents in Matthew 25:13. The women are taught to initiate various income generating projects such as dressmaking, cross-border trading and vending. Musoni affirms that most women in ZAOGA FIF drive their own brand new cars, they own magnificent houses and they live modestly, all because of their profits from these talents. In an interview, Pastor Dhlakama (2015) from ZAOGA acknowledged the role of their church, and the ministry through talents, in sustaining women's businesses. She elaborated:

> We are so thankful to our leaders for encouraging talents, as this benefits both the church and the individual. Many women have been able to sustain their families. Above all, our strength from the God of Ezekiel keeps us going; we will never fail, our businesses will never fail.

Precious Stones from Family of God (FOG)

Apart from ZAOGA, the Family of God Church (FOG), through its women's group, the Precious Stones ministry, has proven to be quite valuable to the lives of women. They have been taught to to work hard and be fruitful in their families. According to Togarasei (2005:364), they are "encouraged to emulate the virtuous woman of Proverbs 31:10–31." As such, women support themselves in various projects of fundraising so as to emulate the ideal of the hardworking women. By so doing, they are motivated by their religious beliefs to be financially astute. Togarasei (2005: 364) also identifies the role of this ministry in transforming the economic life of the adherents. According to Togarasei (2005: 364):

> The women provide material and social assistance to those of their group starting a home. They arrange house-warming parties for those moving into new houses, baby welcome parties, birthday parties, 'kitchen top-ups' and funeral assistance. . .The FOG women's ministry has even started the Gemstone Resource Centre meant to assist women getting into small businesses. Women are encouraged to get into businesses to raise money for the church and for themselves. Even those employed elsewhere are encouraged to boost their finances by engaging in other income generation projects. The women are also taught to be presentable every time and everywhere. This is another clear testimony of the modernity of the church. Elaborate hair-dos and make-ups are encouraged in this church. Women are encouraged to put on clothes of 'silk and purple' like the virtuous wife of Proverbs. The women's ministry therefore runs a grooming school where one pays a small fee in order to be trained on how to present oneself as a modern woman.

This is further supported by Biri and Togarasei (2013:87) who argue that:

> Hard work and entrepreneurship were encouraged. Using the example of the virtuous woman in Proverbs 31:10ff, women encouraged each other not to just depend on their husbands for sustenance but to fend for themselves and for others. Since mothers feed the children, the teaching among the women was that, as mothers in Zimbabwe, they needed to feed the nation both physically (by producing agricultural products, for example) and spiritually (by praying for the good of the land). Empowerment lessons were shared as women taught each other how to be productive. Different Pentecostal churches therefore pioneered projects to empower women. Pentecostals created opportunities for employment through running hospitals, schools, hotels, universities. In the discourses of Pentecostal women, this was to demonstrate that Pentecostals, especially the women members, could re-build the nation of Zimbabwe.

One can thus argue that FOG has one of the ministries that has been able to transform the lives of women economically. In an interview, Mrs Mukahuru (2011) acknowledged the ability of the ministry's programmes to capacitate her financially. She said, "Most of us women have not been able to go to school, but we mix with the rich and educated, as we exchange knowledge on how to make money."

Celebration Ministries

One key study that chronicles the church and entrepreneurship, with particular reference to the Celebration Church is the study by Ndhlovu (2012). He notes the significance of 'entrepreneurship as a strategy to mitigate poverty' (2012:31).

Brief Analysis

From these three particular examples, this chapter argues that a Pentecostal ethic continues to propel the spirit of capitalism, or rather an economic culture within Pentecostalism. This argument does not undermine the role of other faiths, and neither does it suggest that all women in business in Zimbabwe are 'powered by faith.' It is from the selected Pentecostals in the study as a whole that one is bound to appreciate the role of their different ministries in 'keeping women going', even, in most instances, when the financial tide goes against them. This presents a new situation, different from that noted by Mupedziswa and Gumbo (2001: 110), where women in the informal sector did not yield much income. According to their study, "the traders were therefore operating not necessarily to improve their socio-economic well-being but to survive on a day to day basis." In this particular study, religion has made a lot of difference, and has allowed the women involved to 'live with dignity' (Mouton et al 2015). As explained by Mrs Mazvita in an interview (2015), "had it not by the encouragement I get from the teachings of our ladies ministry, I could have by now returned to the rural areas." Indeed, Pentecostalism has a unique way of addressing the financial capacity of women. This fulfils the notion that Pentecostalism has enabled women to thrive in amidst challenges (Mapuranga 2012:121). According to Mapuranga (2012:121), with particular reference to the role of Pentecostalism as a survival strategy amongst the youth at the university, "among other reasons, the culture of Pentecostalism was a survival strategy for many...It was a shield, and it provided comfort and solace." Pentecostalism provides a unique ethic for women in business to thrive, despite the challenges of a tough economy.

Conclusion

This study utilises a theoretical approach that identifies a connection between religion and development to understand the relationship between Pentecostalism and the economic empowerment of women in Zimbabwe after 2009. These theories have emerged specifically from the studies stemming from Max Weber and other scholars discussed above. The conclusion drawn from Zimbabwean Pentecostalism is that it has a unique ability to address believers' economic challenges. This is achieved through the gospel of prosperity, and its capability to transform the mentality of its believers to start self-help projects such as "talents," peanut butter making, sewing and knitting amongst others. Just as the Protestant ethic was in part able to give rise to the spirit of capitalism in the West, so too has Pentecostalism been able in part to give rise to the spirit of capitalism in Zimbabwe in the 21st century. Thus, this study concludes that indeed, Pentecostal women in Zimbabwe are 'powered by faith' to become successful entrepreneurs.

References

Akoko, R. M. (2007). *Ask and you will be given: Pentecostalism and the economic crisis in Cameroon*. Leiden: African Studies.

Amanze, J. (2008). "From the periphery to the centre: The radical transformation of Pentecostal-charismatic Christianity in the 20th century" *Studia Historicae Ecclesiasticae* XXXIV, Vol. 34 (2), 1–10.

Asamoah, M.K. (2013). "Penteco/charismatic worldview of prosperity theology," *African Educational Research Journal* Vol. 1(3), 198–208.

Ayegboyin, Deji. (2011). "New Pentecostal Churches and Prosperity in Nigeria," in Afe Adogame, ed., *Who is Afraid of the Holy Spirit? Pentecostalism and Globalization in Africa and Beyond*. Trenton, NJ: Africa World Pr.

Berger, Peter L. (1967). *The Sacred Canopy: Elements of a Sociological Theory of Religion*. Garden City: Doubleday.

———. (2004). "Max Weber is alive and well, and Living in Guatemala: The Protestant Ethic Today." Speech given at a conference entitled "The Norms, Beliefs, and Institutions of Capitalism: Celebrating Weber's Protestant Ethic and the Spirit of Capitalism," in October 2004 at the Center for the Study of Economy & Society. http://www.economyandsociety.org/events/Berger_paper.pdf, accessed 18 March 2012.

Biri, K. (2012). "The Silent Echoing Voice: Aspects of Zimbabwean Pentecostalism and the Quest for Power, Healing and Miracles," *Studia Historiae Ecclesiasticae* 38 - Supplement, 37-55.

Biri, K.and L. Togarasei, (2013) ."...But The One Who Prophesies, Builds The Church," Ezra Chitando, Masiiwa Ragies Gunda and Joachim Kugler (eds.), *Prophets, Profits and the Bible in Zimbabwe*, University of Bamberg Press: Bamberg.

Bourdillon, M.F.C. (1993), *Where are the Ancestors? Changing culture in Zimbabwe*, Harare, University of Zimbabwe Publications.

Brusco, Elizabeth. (2009). "Review: 'Progressive Pentecostalism'?" *Anthropology and Humanism*, Vol. 34, (1), 117–118.

Chitando, E (2013), "Prophets, Profits and Protests: Prosperity Theology and Zimbabwean Gospel Music," in Ezra Chitando, Masiiwa Ragies Gunda and Joachim Kugler (eds.), *Prophets, Profits and the Bible in Zimbabwe*, University of Bamberg Press: Bamberg.

Coleman, James A. (1968). "Church-Sect Typology and Organizational Precariousness." *Sociological Analysis*, Vol. 29 (2), 55–66

Frahm-Arp, M. (2010), *Professional women in South African Pentecostal Charismatic churches*, Leiden: Brill.

Garrard-Burnett, Virginia. (2012). "Neo-Pentecostalism and Prosperity Theology in Latin America: A Religion for Late Capitalist Society," *IBEROAMERICANA: Nordic Journal of Latin American and Caribbean Studies* XLII (1 & 2), 21–34.

Gifford.P. (1988).*The religious right in southern Africa*, Harare: University of Zimbabwe Publications.

Kirby, B, (2014). "Perspectives on Pentecostalism and Socio-Economic Transformation," *Exchange* Vol. 43, 291- 300.

Mapuranga, T.P (2013), "Bargaining with Patriarchy? Women Pentecostal leaders in Zimbabwe," *Fieldwork in Religion*, Vol. 8 (1), 74–91.

———. (2012). 'Youth and the Culture of Pentecostalism as a Survival Strategy for Female Students at the University of Zimbabwe: 2000–2008,' Laweyi, OlatundeBayo and Francesca Ukpokolo Chinyere (eds.), *Space Transformation and Representation: Reflections on University Culture*, Goldline and Jacobs Publishers: New Jersey, 109-122.

Marshall, R., (2010). "The Sovereignty of Miracles:Pentecostal Political Theology in Nigeria," *Constellations* Vol. 17, (2),197-222.

Martin, D., (1990), *Tongues of Fire. The Explosion of Protestantism in Latin America*, Oxford: Blackwell.

———. (2002).*Pentecostalism: The World as Their Parish* . Oxford: Blackwell.

Mate, R., (2002). "Wombs as God's Laboratories: Pentecostal Discourses of Femininity in Zimbabwe," in *Africa: Journal of the International African Institute*,Vol.72 (4), 549-568.

Maxwell, D. (2006). *African Gifts of the Spirit: Pentecostalism and the Rise of a Zimbabwean Transnational Religious Movement*. Harare: Weaver Pr.

———. (1998). "'Delivered from the Spirit of Poverty': Pentecostalism, Prosperity and Modernity in Zimbabwe," *Journal of Religion in Africa* 28(4), 350-373.

Miller, Donald E., and Tetsunao Yamamori. (2007). *Global Pentecostalism: The New Face of Christian Social Engagement*. Berkeley: University of California Press.

Mouton, E, Kapuma Getrude, Hansen, Len and Togo Thomas (eds.), (2015).*Living with Dignity: African Perspectives on Gender Equality*, Sun Press: Stellenbosch EFSA Institute.

Mupedziswa R., and Gumbo, P. (2001).*Women and Informal Traders in Harare and the struggle for survival in an Environment of Economic Reforms*, Research Report no 117, Uppsalla: Nordiska Afrikainstitutet.

Musoni, P. (2013) "African Pentecostalism and Sustainable Development: A Study of Zimbabwe Assemblies of God Africa Forward in Faith Church," in *International Journal of Humanities and Social Science Invention*, Vol. 2 (10), 75-82.

Ndlovu, Lovemore. (2012). "Pentecostalism as a Form of Protest Movement against Economic Decline and Tyranny: The Case of Celebration Church in Zimbabwe," *Serbian Political Thought* 5(1), 25-47.

Nogueira-Godsey, T., (2012). "Weberian Sociology and the Study of Pentecostalism: Historical Patterns and Prospects for the Future," *Journal for the Study of Religion*, Vol. 25, (2,) 51-69.

Redding, S. Gordon. (1990).*The Spirit of Chinese Capitalism*. Berlin: W. de Gruyter.

Stokes, R. G. (1975). "Afrikaner Calvinism and Economic Action: The Weberian Thesis in South Africa." *American Journal of Sociology* , Vol.81 (1), 62-81.

Togarasei, Lovemore. (2010). "Churches for the Rich? Pentecostalism and Elitism," in Lovemore Togarasei and Ezra Chitando, eds., *Faith in the City: The Role and Place of Religion in Harare*. Uppsala: Swedish Science Pr.

Togarasei Lovemore (2005). "Modern Pentecostalism As An Urban Phenomenon: The Case of the Family Of God Church In Zimbabwe" in *Exchange: Journal of Missiological and Ecumenical Research*, Vol.34, No.4, 2005, 368-370.

Weber, M. (1958).*The Protestant Ethic and the Spirit of Capitalism*.Translated by Talcott Parsons. New York: Scribner.

Zimunya, C and J. Gwara (2013), "Pentecostalism, Prophets and the Distressing Zimbabwean Milieu," in Ezra Chitando, Masiiwa Ragies Gunda and Joachim Kugler (eds.), *Prophets, Profits and the Bible in Zimbabwe*, University of Bamberg Press: Bamberg.

Interviews

The author sought authority to use real names of Interviewees.

Dhlakama, G., 2013 a Pastor with ZAOGA.

Mazvita R., 2015, a member within Pentecostalism with big business in the clothing industry.

Mukahuru, J., 2011, a member of FOG.

Murwira T., 2015, a member of ZAOGA.

Mutezo,T., 2014, a member of the Prophetic Healing and Deliverance Ministry.

Bibliography

Abdullah, M.A. and Bakar M.H. *Small and Medium Enterprises in Asian Pacific Countries: Roles and Issues,* New York: Nova Science Publishers, Inc, 2000.

Adelegan, F. *Nigeria's Leading Lights of the Gospel Revolutionaries in Worldwide Christianity,* Bloomington: West Bow Press, 2013.

Akoko R. M. "New Pentecostalism in the Wake of The Economic Crisis In Cameroon," *Nordic Journal Of African Studies* 11(3), 2002, 359-376.

Akoko, R. M. *Ask and you will be given: Pentecostalism and the economic crisis in Cameroon.* Leiden: African Studies, 2007.

Alexander, J. "The Historiography of Land in Zimbabwe: Strengths, Silences, and Questions" in: *Safundi: The Journal of South African and American Studies,* Vol. 8(2), 2007, 183-198.

Allaman, J., Geiger, S. and Musisi, N. *Women in African Colonial Histories,* Bloomington: Indiana University Press, 2002.

Amanze, J. "From the periphery to the centre: The radical transformation of Pentecostal-charismatic Christianity in the 20th century" *Studia Historicae Ecclesiasticae* XXXIV, Vol. 34 (2), 2008, 1-10.

Asamoah, M.K. "Penteco/Charismatic Worldview of Prosperity Theology," *.African Educational Research Journal,* Vol. 1(3), 2013, 198-208.

Asamoah-Gyadu, J.K. "'Born of Water and the Spirit': Pentecostal/Charismatic Christianity in Africa" in: O.U. Kalu (Ed.) African Christianity, 2005, 388-409, Available on: http://repository.up.ac.za/bitstream/handle/2263/21579/016_Chapter15_p388-409.pdf?sequence=17, Accessed: 10 March 2015.

Asamoah-Gyadu, K. "African Pentecostal/Charismatic Christianity: An Overview." *Category: Themed,* Issue 8, 2006.

Attanasi, K. The Plurality of Prosperity Theology and Pentecostalisms'.In Attanasi, K. & Yong, A. (eds.), *Pentecostalism and Prosperity.* New York: Palgrave MacMillan, 2012, 1-19.

Ayegboyin, Deji. "New Pentecostal Churches and Prosperity in Nigeria," in Afe Adogame, ed., *Who is Afraid of the Holy Spirit? Pentecostalism and Globalization in Africa and Beyond.* Trenton, NJ: Africa World Pr, 2011.

Bauer, J. *The Flight of the Pheonix: Investing in Zimbabwe's Rise from the Ashes during the Colonial Global Debt Crisis,* Berlin: epubli, 2013.

Berger, Peter L. *The Sacred Canopy: Elements of a Sociological Theory of Religion.* Garden City: Doubleday, 1967.

Berger, Peter, L. "Max Weber is alive and well, and Living in Guatemala: The Protestant Ethic Today." Speech given at a conference entitled "The Norms, Beliefs, and

BIBLIOGRAPHY

Institutions of Capitalism: Celebrating Weber's Protestant Ethic and the Spirit of Capitalism," in October 2004 at the Center for the Study of Economy & Society. http://www.economyandsociety.org/events/Berger_paper.pdf, accessed 18 March 2012.

Biri, K. "The Silent Echoing Voice: Aspects of Zimbabwean Pentecostalism and the Quest for Power, Healing and Miracles." *Studia, Historiae Ecclesiasticae Supplement*, Vol. 38, 2102, 37–55.

Biri, K.and L. Togarasei, ". . .But The One Who Prophesies, Builds The Church," Ezra Chitando, Masiiwa Ragies Gunda and Joachim Kugler (eds.), *Prophets, Profits and the Bible in Zimbabwe*, University of Bamberg Press: Bamberg, 2013.

Bond, P. and Manyanya, M. *Zimbabwe's Plunge: Exhausted Nationalism, Neoliberalism, and the Search for Social Justice*, Harare: Weaver Press, 2003.

Bourdillon, M.F.C., *Where are the Ancestors? Changing culture in Zimbabwe*, Harare: University of Zimbabwe Publications, 1993.

Brown, M. E. *Famine Early Warning Systems and Remote Sensing Data*, Berlin: Springer Science and Business Media, 2008.

Brusco, Elizabeth. "Review: 'Progressive Pentecostalism'?" *Anthropology and Humanism*, Vol. 34, (1), 2009, 117–118.

Carver, L.C. "The Founding of the Apostolic Faith Work in Zimbabwe and its Growth in Southern Africa," 1987, Available on: www.hatnews.org, Accessed: 20 April 2015.

Charantimath, P. M. *Entrepreneurship Development and Small Business Enterprise*, New Delhi: Pearson Education, 2006.

Cheater, A. *The Anthropology of Power*, New York: Routledge, 2003.

Chitando, E. "African Instituted Churches in Southern Africa: Paragons of regional Integration. *African Journal of International Affairs*," Vol, 7, Nos 1 and 2, 2004, 117–132.

Chitando, E. "Deliverance and Sanctified Passports: Prophetic Activities amidst Uncertainty in Harare," in Haram, A.and Yamba, C. B. (eds.), *Dealing with uncertainty in contemporary African lives*. Nordiska African Institute, 2009.

Chitando, E. "Prophets, Profits and Protests: Prosperity Theology and Zimbabwean Gospel Music," in Ezra Chitando, Masiiwa Ragies Gunda and Joachim Kugler (eds.), *Prophets, Profits and the Bible in Zimbabwe*, University of Bamberg Press: Bamberg. 2013.

Chitando, E. *Singing Culture: A Study of Gospel Music in Zimbabwe*: Uppsala: Nordic Africa Institute, 2002.

Chitando, E., Manyonganise, M. and Mlambo, O.. 'Young, Male and Polished: Masculinities, Generational Shifts and Pentecostal Prophets in Zimbabwe'. In Chitando, E., Gunda, R.M. & Kugler, J. (eds.) *Prophets, Profits and the Bible in Zimbabwe*. Bamberg: University of Bamberg Press, 2013.

Chiweza, D. *Out of the Rabble: Ending the Global Economic Crisis by Understanding the Zimbabwean Experience*, Bloomington: iUniverse, 2013.

Chopamba, L. *The Struggle for Economic Support of the Indigenous Women Business in Zimbabwe*, Bloomington : XLIBRIS Corporation, 2010.

Churches in Manicaland. *The Truth Will Make You Free: A Compendium of Christian Social Teachings*, Mutare: Churches in Manicaland, 2006.

Coleman, James A. "Church-Sect Typology and Organizational Precariousness." *Sociological Analysis* , Vol. 29 (2), 1968, 55–66

BIBLIOGRAPHY

Coughlin, J.H. and Thomas, A. R. *The rise of Women Entrepreneurs: People, Processes and Global Trend,* Westport: Greenwood Publishing Group, 2002.

Cox, H.G. *Fire from Heaven: The Rise of Pentecostal Spirituality and the Reshaping of Religion in the Twenty-First Century,* Reading: Addison-Wesley, 1996.

D'Cruz, P. *Family Care in HIV/AIDS: Exploring Lived Experience,* New Delhi: Sage Publications, 2004.

Dash, A. in Franz, H. et al. (eds), *Challenge Social Innovation: Potentials for Business, Social Entrepreneurship, Welfare and Civil Society,* New York: Springer, 2012.

Derera E. et al, in Kubacki, K. *Ideas in Marketing: Finding the New and Polishing the Old: Proceedings of the 2013 Academy of Marketing Science,* New York: Springer International Publishing, 2014.

Doxtader, E. and Villa-Vicencio, C. *Through Fire with Water: The Roots of Division and the Potential for Reconciliation in Africa,* Claremont: New Africa Books, 2003.

Dube, M.W. *Postcolonial Feminist Interpretation of the Bible,* Danvers: Chalice Press, 2000.

Durran, M. *Fundraising for Churches,* London: Canterbury Press, 2003.

Dwivedi, D.N. *Managerial Economics, 7 E,* Noida: Vikas Publishing House, 2009.

Europa Publications, Murison, K. (ed), *South of the Sahara 2004,* London: Psychology Press, 2003.

Eyre, Banning, *Playing with Fire,* Copenhagen: Freemuse handy-Print, 2001.

Frahm-Arp, M. *Professional Women in South African Pentecostal Charismatic Churches,* Leiden: Brill, 2010.

Frahm-Arp, M. "African Pentecostalism and Gender Roles," in Clarke, C.R. (ed.) *Pentecostal Theology in Africa.* Eugene: Wipf and Stock Publishers, 2014.

Friedmann, J.L.'Liberating Domesticity: Women and the Home in Orthodox Judaism and Latin American Pentecostalism', *Journal of Religion and Society,* Vol. 10, 2008, 2–16.

Gabaitse, Rosinah M. "Pentecostal Hermeneutics and Marginalisation of Women," *Scriptura* 114(1), 2015, 1–12.

Gabay, C. & Death, C., *Critical Perspectives on African Politics, Liberal Inventions, State building and Civil society,* New York: Routledge, 2014.

Gaidzanwa, R. *Voting with their Feet: A Study of Zimbabwe Doctors and Nurses in the Era of Structural Adjustment Programme,* Uppsala: Nordiska Afrikainstitutet, 1999.

Gandhi, L. *Post colonial Theory: A Critical Introduction,* Edinburgh: Edinburgh University Press, 1998.

Garrard-Burnett, Virginia. "Neo-Pentecostalism and Prosperity Theology in Latin America: A Religion for Late Capitalist Society," *IBEROAMERICANA: Nordic Journal of Latin American and Caribbean Studies XLII* (1 & 2), 2012, 21–34.

Gbote, E.Z.M. and S.T. Kgatla. "Prosperity Gospel: A Missiological Assessment" University of Pretoria, *HTS Teologiese Studies/Theological Studies* 70, (1), 2014, 1–10.

Gifford, P. "Some Recent Developments in African Christianity," *African Affairs,* Vol. 93 (373), 1994, 513–534.

Gifford, P. *The Religious Right in Southern Africa,* Harare: Baobab Books, 1988.

Gifford, P. *Ghana's New Christianity: Pentecostalism in a globalizing African Economy,* London: C Hurst & Co Publishers, 2004.

Gifford, Paul. "African Christianity: A New and Foreign Element in African Christianity," *Religion* 20, 1990, 273–288.

Gono, G. *Zimbabwe's Casino Economy: Extraordinary Measures for Extraordinary Challenges,* Harare: ZPH Publishers, 2008.

Bibliography

Gopal, G. & Salim, M. *Gender and Law: Eastern Africa Speaks: Proceedings of The Conference Organized by the World Bank & Economic Commission for Africa*, Washington: W B Publications, 1998.

Guti, E.H. *History of ZAOGA, Forward in Faith*, Harare: EGEA Publications, 1999.

Guti, E.H. *The Church and Political Responsibility*, Harare: EGEA Publications, 1994.

Hackett, R.I.J. "Women and New Religious Movements in Africa," in U. King (ed.) *Religion and Gender*, Oxford: Blackwell, 1995.

Hadebe, N.M. "Healing and HIV in Pentecostal Churches" in: E. Chitando and C. Klagba (Eds.) *In the Name of Jesus!: Healing in the Age of HIV*, Geneva: WCC Publications, 2013.

Heaton, T., James, S. & Oheneba-Sakyi, Y. 'Religion and Socio-economic Attainment in Ghana,' *Review of Religious Research*, Vol. 51(1), 2009, 71–86.

Kadenge, M. and Mavunga, G. "The Zimbabwe Crisis as Captured in Shona Metaphor," *Journal of African Cultural Studies*, Vol. 23(2), 2011, 153–164.

Kalu, O. U. 'A Discursive Interpretation of African Pentecostalism'.*Fides et Historia* 41(1), 2009, 71–90.

Kalu, O.U. "'Globecalisation' and Religion: The Pentecostal Model in Contemporary Africa" in: J.L. Cox and G. ter Haar (Eds.) *Uniquely African?: African Christian Identity from Cultural and Historical Perspectives*, Trenton: Africa World Press, Inc., 2003.

Kanyenze, G. *Beyond the Enclave: Towards a Pro-Poor Inclusive Development Strategy*, Harare: Weaver Press, 2011.

King, D. W. *This Business of Gospel Music: How to make money and achieve success in today's United States, Canada and United Kingdom Gospel Music Industry*, Gospel knowledge Books, 2012.

Kirby, B. "Perspectives on Pentecostalism and Socio-Economic Transformation," *Exchange* Vol. 43, 2014, 291- 300.

Lechner, F.J., & Boli, J. *World Culture: Origins and Consequences*. Oxford: Blackwell Publishing, 2005.

Lupinacci, A. S. *Women and Business Ownership: Entrepreneurs in Dallas, Texas, Garland Studies and Entrepreneurship*, New York: Taylor and Francis, 1998.

Majawa, C.C.A. *The Holy Spirit and Charismatic Renewal in Africa and Beyond: Pneumatological Considerations*, Nairobi: Creations Enterprises, 2006.

Manase, I. "Representations of post-2000 Zimbabwean Economic Migrancy in Petina Gappah's *An Elegy for Easterly* and Brian Chikwava's *Harare North*," *Journal of Black Studies*, Vol. 45(1), 2014, 59–76.

Manyonganise, M. 'Pentecostals Responding to Gender-based Violence: The Case of the United Family International Church in Harare'. In Chitando, E. and Chirongoma, S. (eds.) *Justice Not Silence: Churches Facing Sexual and Gender-based Violence*. Stellenbosch: EFSA, 2013

Maposa, R.S. 'Land to the Landless? Theological Reflections on Some Churches to the Land Reform program in Zimbabwe, 2000–2012, in *Africana*, Vol.6 (1), 2012,78–109.

Mapuranga T.P . "Youth and the culture of Pentecostalism as a Survival Strategy for Female Students at the University of Zimbabwe, 2000–2008," in *Space Transformation and Representation: Reflections on University Culture*, Olatunde Bayo Lawuyi and Chinyere Ukpokolo (eds.), New Jersey: Goldline and Jacobs Publishers, 2012.

BIBLIOGRAPHY

Mapuranga, P., Chitando, E., and Gunda, M.R. "Studying the United Family International Church in Zimbabwe: The Case for Applying Multiple Approaches to the Study of Religion and Religious Phenomena," in: E. Chitando, M.R. Gunda and J. Kugler (eds.) *Prophets, Profits and the Bible in Zimbabwe*, Bamberg: UBP, 2013.

Mapuranga, T.P. 'Surviving the Urban Jungle: African Initiated Churches and Women's Socio-Economic Coping Strategies in Harare 2000-2010', in E. Chitando, J. Kugler and M.R Gunda (eds.), *Multiplying In The Spirit: African Initiated Churches In Zimbabwe*, Bamberg: Bamberg University Press, 2014.

Mapuranga, T.P. "Bargaining with Patriarchy?: Women Pentecostal Leaders in Zimbabwe," *Fieldwork in Religion*, Vol. 8(1), 2013,74-91.

Markovic, M. R. in Markovic M.R. (ed) *The Perspective of Women's Entrepreneurship in the Age of Globalisation*, Charlotte: IAP, 2007.

Marshall, R. "The Sovereignty of Miracles:Pentecostal Political Theology in Nigeria," *Constellations* Vol. 17, (2), 2010, 197–222.

Martin, D. *Pentecostalism: The World as Their Parish* . Oxford: Blackwell, 2002.

Martin, D. *Tongues of Fire. The Explosion of Protestantism in Latin America*, Oxford: Blackwell, 1990.

Masenya, M. The Woman of Worth in Proverbs 31:10-31: Reread through a Bosadi (Womanhood lens), 2011, http://ghfe.org/wp-content/uploads/2013/02/gbfe-jahrbuch-2011-masenya) accessed on 15 April 2015.

Massey, D. *For Space*, London: Sage, 2005.

Massey, D. *Space, Place and Gender*, Cambridge: Polity Press, 1994.

Mate, R. "Wombs as God's Laboratories: Pentecostal Discourses of Femininity in Zimbabwe," in *Africa: Journal of the International African Institute*, Vol. 72 (4), 2002, 549–568.

Mauchi, F.N, Mutengezanwa, M. and Damiyano, D. 'Challenges Faced by Women Entrepreneurs: A Case Study of Mashonaland Central Province, *International Journal of Development and Sustainability*, Vol 3.3, 2014, 466–480.

Maxwell, D. "Catch the Cockerel before Dawn: Pentecostalism and Politics in Post Colonial Zimbabwe," in *Africa* Vol. (LXX), no.(2), 2000, 249–277.

Maxwell, D. "'Delivered from the Spirit of Poverty?': Pentecostalism, Prosperity and Modernity in Zimbabwe," *Journal of Religion in Africa*, Vol. 28(3), 1998, 350–373.

Maxwell, D. "The Durawall of Faith: Pentecostal Spirituality in neo-Liberal Zimbabwe," *Journal of Religion in Africa*, 35, no 14-32, 2005.

Maxwell, D. *African Gifts of the Spirit: Pentecostalism and the Rise of a Zimbabwean Transnational Religious Movement*. Harare: Weaver Pr, 2006.

Maxwell, David. "Review Article: In Defence of African Creativity," *Journal of Religion in Africa* 30(4), 2000, 468–481.

Mboko, S. and Smith-Hunter, A. "Zimbabwe Women Business Owners: Survival Strategies and Implications for Growth," *Journal of Applied Business and Economics*, vol. 11 (2), 2009, 82–104.

Michael, R. *The Gospel Music according to Saint Ralph Michael*, I AM-THAT-I AM publishing company, 2005.

Miller, D.E., Holland, S., Johnson, D. and Fendall, L, *Seeking Peace in Africa: Stories from African Peacemakers*, Pennsylvania: Cascadia Publishing House, 2004.

Miller, Donald E., and Tetsunao Yamamori. *Global Pentecostalism: The New Face of Christian Social Engagement*. Berkeley: University of California Press, 2007.

Bibliography

Mlambo, A. and Raftopoulos, B. "The Regional Dimensions of Zimbabwe's Multi-Layered Crisis: An Analysis," 2010, Downloaded from: http//www.iese.ac.mz/lib/publication/proelit/Alois_Mlambo.pdf, Accessed: 11.12.13.

Moila, P.M. *Challenging Issues in Christianity*, Pretoria: Unisa Press, 2002.

Mombi, G. "Impact of the Prosperity Gospel in the Assemblies of God Churches of Papua New Guinea," *Melanesian Journal of Theology*, Vol. 25, No.1, 2009,32–58.

Mouton, E, Kapuma Getrude, Hansen, Len and Togo Thomas (eds.), *Living with Dignity: African Perspectives on Gender Equality*, Sun Press: Stellenbosch EFSA Institute, 2015.

Msipah *et al*, "Entrepreneurial Training Needs Analysis in Small-Scale Artisanal Engineering Business in Zimbabwe: A case study of Mashonaland West Province," *Journal of Sustainable Development in Africa*, Vol.15 (2), 2013, 81–98.

Munyikwa, H. in Hudson *et al* (eds), *Peace, Conflict and Identity: Multidisplinary Approaches to research*, Bilbao, University of Deusto, 2009.

Mupedziswa R., and Gumbo, P. *Women and Informal Traders in Harare and the struggle for survival in an Environment of Economic Reforms*, Research Report no 117, Uppsalla: Nordiska Afrikainstitutet, 2001.

Musoni, P. "African Pentecostalism and Sustainable Development: A Study of Zimbabwe Assemblies of God Africa Forward in Faith Church," in *International Journal of Humanities and Social Science Invention*, Vol. 2 (10), 2013, 75–82.

Muzvidziwa, V.N. "Cross-Border Trade: A Strategy for Climbing out of Poverty in Masvingo, Zimbabwe," *Zambezia*, XXV (i), 1998, 29–58.

Mwaura, P.N. 'Gender and Power in African Christianity: African Instituted Churches and Pentecostal Churches,' in Kalu, O.U. (ed.) *African Christianity: An African Story*. New Jersey: Africa World Press, 2007.

Naude, W. A. and Havenga, J. J. D. (2005), "An overview of African entrepreneurship and small business research," Journal of Small Business and Entrepreneurship, Vol. 18, 101–120.

Ncube, M. "Employment, Unemployment and the Evolution of labour policy in Zimbabwe," *Zambezia*, XXVVII, (ii), 2000, 161–193.

Ndlovu, Lovemore. "Pentecostalism as a Form of Protest Movement against Economic Decline and Tyranny: The Case of Celebration Church in Zimbabwe," *Serbian Political Thought* 5(1), 2012, 25–47.

Njoh, A.J. *Tradition, Culture and Development in Africa: Historical Lessons for Modern Development Planning*, Surrey: Ashgate Pubishing Ltd, 2006.

Nogueira-Godsey, T. "Weberian Sociology and the Study of Pentecostalism: Historical Patterns and Prospects for the Future," *Journal for the Study of Religion*, Vol. 25, (2,) 2012, 51–69.

Oduyoye, M.A. and Kanyoro, M.R.A. *The Will to Arise: Women, Tradition and the Church in Africa*, New York: Maryknoll, 1992.

Omenyo, C.N. "African Pentecostalism," in Robeck, C.M. & Yong, A. (ed.), *The Cambridge Companion to Pentecostalism*. USA: Cambridge University Press, 2014.

Oyakhilome, A. *Wisdom for Women*, Lagos: Love World Publication, 1998.

Oyakhilome, C. *How To Make Your Faith Work*, Lagos: Love World Publishing Ministry, 2007.

Oyakhilome, C. *Rhapsody of Realities. . . A Daily Devotional*, Lagos: Love World Publishing, 2015.

BIBLIOGRAPHY

Parsitau, D. "Agents of Gendered Change: Empowerment, Salvation and Gendered Transformation in Urban Kenya," in Freeman, D. (ed.) *Pentecostalism and Development: Churches, NGOs and Social Change in Africa*. New York: Palgrave Macmillan, 2012.

Porter, R. B. et al, *Geographies of Development: An Introduction to Development Studies*, 3rd Edition, Essex: Pearson Education Limited, 2008.

Raftopoulos, B."The Crisis in Zimbabwe, 1998-2008," Raftopoulos, B. and Mlambo, A. (eds.), *Becoming Zimbabwe: A History from the Pre-colonial Period to 2008*, Harare: Weaver Press, 2009.

Redding, S. Gordon. *The Spirit of Chinese Capitalism*. Berlin: W. de Gruyter, 1990.

Rodney, W. *How Europe Underdeveloped Africa*, Dar es Salaam: EAP, 1972

Shoko, T. & Chiwara, A. 'The Prophetic Figure in Zimbabwean Religions: A Comparative Analysis of Prophet Makandiwa of the United Family International Church (UFIC) and the N'anga in African Traditional Religion. In Chitando, E., Gunda, R.M. & Kugler, J. (eds.), *Prophets, Profits and the Bible in Zimbabwe*. Bamberg: University of Bamberg Press, 2013.

Shoko, T. "Healing in Hear the Word Ministries Pentecostal Church in Zimbabwe," in Westerlund D. (ed), *Global Pentecostalism*, London: I.B. Tauris Publishers, 2009.

Shoko, T. "Independent Church Healing: The Case of St Elijah Cum Enlightenment School of the Holy Spirit in Zimbabwe." *Studia Historiae Ecclesiasticae*, Vol XXX11 (3), 2006, 130-153.

Shoko, T. "'My Bone Shall Rise Again': War Veterans, Spirits and Land Reform in Zimbabwe," African Studies Centre, Leiden: ASC Working Paper, No. 68, 2006.

Sibanda, F. *African Blitzkrieg in Zimbabwe: Phenomenological Reflections on Shona Beliefs on Lightning*, Saarbrucken: Lambert Academic Publishers, 2011.

Sibanda, F. and Maposa, R.S. "Beyond the Third Chimurenga?: Theological Reflections on the Land Reform Programme in Zimbabwe, 2000-2010," *The Journal of Pan African Studies*, Vol. 6(8), 2014, 54-74.

Sibanda, F. and Maposa, R.S. in Chitando, E. Gunda, M. R and Kugler, J. *Multiplying the Spirit: African Initiated Churches in Zimbabwe*, Bamberg, Bamberg Press, 2014.

Sibanda, F., and Maposa, R.S. (2013) "Beasts of Burden?: Women in HIV & AIDS Contexts in the United Church of Christ in Zimbabwe," in: E. Chitando and S. Chirongoma (Eds.) *Justice not Silence: Churches Facing Sexual and Gender-based Violence*, Stellenbosch: AFSA, 2013.

Sibanda, F., Makahamadze, T. and Maposa, R.S. "Hawks and Doves: The Impact of Operation Murambatsvina on Johane Marange Apostolic Church in Zimbabwe," *Exchange: Journal of Theological and Missiological Studies*, Vol.37, 2008, 68-85

Sibanda, F., Marevesa, T. and Muzambi, P. "Miracles or Magic?: Theological Reflections on the Healing Ministry in Pentecostal Churches in Zimbabwe" *JIARM*, Vol. 1 (8) 2013, 248-261.

Simango, J. "ZAOGA (FIF)'s Story in Fundraising: Assessing the Impact of Working Talents for God's Purpose and Organizational Development at Hatfield District," Diploma Project Submitted at Africa Leading Development Network, Harare; June 2012.

Smith, B.N. *The Oxford Encyclopaedia of Women in World History*, Vol 4, Oxford: University Press. 2008.

BIBLIOGRAPHY

Soothill, J. 2014. "Gender and Pentecostalism in Africa," in Lindhardt, L. (ed.) *Pentecostalism in Africa: Presence and Impact of Pneumatic Christianity in Post-Colonial Society*. Leiden: Brill Academic Publishers, 2014.

Spinks, C. "Panacea or Painkiller? The Impact of Pentecostal Christianity on Women in Africa" *Annual Journal of Women for Women International*, Vol.1, No.1, 2003, 20-25.

Stokes, R. G. "Afrikaner Calvinism and Economic Action: The Weberian Thesis in South Africa." *American Journal of Sociology*, Vol.81 (1), 1975, 62-81.

Taringa, N.T and Mapuranga, T.P. "Pluralism and Islam: A historical and Sociological Analysis." in, *Faith in the City: the Role and Place of Religion in Harare*, L Togarasei and E Chitando (eds.), Uppsala: Swedish Science Press, 2010.

The Kairos Document. *Challenges to the Church: A Theological Comment to the Political Crisis in South Africa*, Gweru: Mambo Press, 1985.

Todaro, M.P. and Smith, S.C. *Economic Development*, 11th Edition, Essex: Pearson Education Limited, 2011.

Togarasei Lovemore. "Modern Pentecostalism As An Urban Phenomenon: The Case of the Family Of God Church In Zimbabwe" in *Exchange: Journal of Missiological and Ecumenical Research*, Vol.34, No.4, 2005, 368-370.

Togarasei, L."Churches for the Rich? Pentecostalism and Elitism" in: L. Togarasei and E. Chitando (eds.) *Faith in the City: The Role and Place of Religion in Harare*, Uppsala: Swedish Science Press, 2010.

Togarasei, L. "The Pentecostal Gospel of Prosperity in African Contexts of Poverty: An Appraisal," *Exchange*, Vol. 40, 2011, 336-350.

Togarasei, Lovemore. "Churches for the Rich? Pentecostalism and Elitism," in Lovemore Togarasei and Ezra Chitando, eds., *Faith in the City: The Role and Place of Religion in Harare*. Uppsala: Swedish Science Pr, 2010.

Togarasei, Lovemore. "The Pentecostal Gospel of Prosperity in African Contexts of Poverty: An Appraisal," *Exchange* 40(4), 2011, 336-350.

Van Klinken, Adriaan. "God's World is not an Animal Farm – Or is it? A Catachrestic Translation of Gender Equality in African Pentecostalism," *Religion and Gender* 3(2), 2013 240-258.

Vengeyi O. "Gona and the Bible among Indigenous Pentecostal Churches of Zimbabwe: A Comparative Approach," in Gunda, M.R (ed), *From Text to Practice The Role of The Bible in the Daily Living of African People Today*, BiAS 4, Bamberg: University of Bamberg Press, 2011.

Verstraelen, F.J. *Zimbabwean Realities and Christian Responses*, Gweru: Mambo Press, 1998.

Vossenburg, S. *Women Entrepreneurship Promotion in Developing Countries: What Explains the Gender Gap in Entrepreneurship how to close it?* Maastricht, Maastricht School of Management, 2013.

Weber, M.*The Protestant Ethic and the Spirit of Capitalism*.Translated by Talcott Parsons. New York: Scribner, 1958.

Zeidan, S.and Bahrami, S. "Women Entrepreneurship in GCC: A framework to Address Challenges and Promote Participation in a Regional Context," *International Journal of Business and Social Science*, Vol. 12 (2), 2011, 100-107.

Zimunya, C and J. Gwara. "Pentecostalism, Prophets and the Distressing Zimbabwean Milieu," in Ezra Chitando, Masiiwa Ragies Gunda and Joachim Kugler (eds.), *Prophets, Profits and the Bible in Zimbabwe*, University of Bamberg Press: Bamberg, 2013.

Zindi, F. *The Pop-Music Work Book: Zimbabwe Versus the World*, Harare: Zindisc Publications. 2003.

www.ingramcontent.com/pod-product-compliance
Lightning Source LLC
Chambersburg PA
CBHW072143160426
43197CB00012B/2224